Vegan Made Easy

130 Tasty Recipes That Anyone Can Cook!

Anja Cass

www.CookingWithPlants.com

This book is dedicated to my loving son, my parents, family and friends, who have all given me ongoing motivation to get this cookbook started... and ultimately finished!! And finally, this is also dedicated to my wonderful online supporters who have been patiently waiting for me to bring this book to fruition.

Thank you all!

CONTENTS

MEASUREMENTS

The recipes in this book have been tested with metric measurements so some variations may occur. Please note that my recipes are quite forgiving in terms of exact measurements and for your reference I measure as follows: 1 cup = 250ml | 1 tbs = 20ml | 1 tsp = 5ml. Happy cooking... and eating!

BREAKFAST 6
Date Banana Porridge Smoothie. 8
High Energy Breakfast Smoothie 8
Soy Yogurt 9
Creamed Vanilla Rice Pudding 10
Polenta Porridge with Apricot Drizzle. 11
Baklava Quinoa Porridge 12
No Cook Buckwheat Porridge 13
Sweet French Toast. 14
Savory French Toast. 15
Tofu Scramble. 16
Breakfast Couscous Bites 17
Two Ingredient Waffles 18
Two Ingredient Pancakes 19
Coconut Chia Fruit Bowl 20
"Eggy" Breakfast Muffins. 21
Potato Hash Browns. 22
Chickpea Omelette. 23
Homemade Baked Beans 24
Zucchini Corn Fritters. 25
Lemon Blueberry Muffins 26
Almond Chai Latte. 27

MAIN MEALS. 28
Pizza in a Pan. 30
No Knead Pizza. 31
Gluten Free Quinoa Crusted Pizza. 32
Mac & "Cheese". 33
Potato Crusted Quiche 34
Mediterranean Polenta Stacks 35
Creamy Potato Broccoli Bake 36
Homemade Gnocchi 37
Sweet Potato Falafel Burgers 38

Hearty Mushroom Lentil Burgers. 39
Lasagne Roll Up Bake 40
Cabbage Terrine 41
Spiced Pumpkin Soup + Cashew Cream . . .42
Blend, Heat & Eat Tomato Soup 43
Smoky Leek & Potato Soup 44
Creamy Pumpkin Mint Pea Risotto 45
Lasagne Style Potato Bake 46
Vegan Ground "Beef". 47
Shepherd's Pie. 48
Stuffed Mushrooms 49
Homemade Marinara Sauce. 50
Eggplant Bolognese 51
Vegetable Black Bean Loaf 52
Potato & Vegetable Polenta Slice. 53
Stuffed Red Peppers. 54
Crumbed "No Fish" Fillets 55
Greek Style Herbed Koftas 56
Sunflower Seed Falafels. 57
One Pot Mexican Rice 58
Jackfruit Peri Peri Skewers + Salsa. 59
Potato & Lentil Dahl. 60
Curried Singapore Noodles 61
Curry Fried Rice 62
No Cook Asian Stir fry. 63
Asian Chestnut Noodle Stir Fry. 64
Baked Rice Paper Pockets 65
Dumplings in Hearty Asian Broth. 66
Thai Red Curry 67
Tofu Scramble Fried Rice. 68
Satay Noodles 69

SNACKS & SIDES 70

Cashew "Cheese".........................72
Almond "Cheese" 73
Nut Free Smoked Paprika "Cheese" 74
Halloumi "Cheese" 75
Nut Free "Cheese" Sauce................76
No Oil Seasoned Fries 77
Herbed Mash Potatoes..................78
Oven Roasted Baked Potatoes 79
Lemon Potatoes 80
Creamy Lemon Dijon Potato Salad 81
Creamy Cauliflower....................82
Middle Eastern Cauliflower 83
Vegetable Parcels......................84
Mini Quiches..........................85
Asparagus Puffs 86
Chili Tofu Lettuce Cups 87
No Oil Hummus 88
Greek Spiced Eggplant Hummus 89
Rustic Bread Sticks.................... 90
Maple Spiced Oven Roasted Nuts........91

CONDIMENTS 92

Salt Free Garlic & Herb Seasoning 94
Almond Parmesan "Cheese".............95
Chargrilled Red Pepper Pesto 96
Tzatziki 97
Smoky Red Bell Pepper Dip.............98
Guacamole........................... 99
Oil Free Vegan Mayonnaise 100
Cashew Sour Cream...................101
White Sauce..........................102
Rich Brown Gravy 103
Onion Gravy 104
Mushroom Gravy 105
Instant Cheesy Herb & Garlic Sauce 106
Creamy Garlic Sauce 107
5 minute Curry Sauce 108
Spicy Tomato Ketchup 109

Peanut Dipping Sauce 110
Hoisin Sauce 111
Sweet Chili Chutney....................112
Sweet Chili Dressing 113
Creamy Italian Dressing 114
Caesar Dressing.......................115
Caper Mustard Vinaigrette 116
Orange Tahini Dressing.................117
Asian Miso Dressing....................118
Chili Lime Dressing 119
No "Fish" Sauce.......................120
Sticky Oriental Reduction 121
Balsamic Glaze 122
Pineapple "Honey"....................123

DESSERTS......................... 124

Papaya Fruit Salad with Chia 126
Oven Roasted Stone Fruit...............127
Apple Crumble 128
Banana Creme Brulee 129
Banana Choc Chip Pan-Cake...........130
Chocolate Fudge Cup Cake 131
Chocolate Fudge Brownies.............132
Choc Chip Cookies....................133
Gluten Free Banana Bread 134
Sticky Date Muffins....................135
No Bake Carrot Cake Muffins...........136
Frosted Sweet Potato Cupcakes.........137
Baked Lemon "Cheesecake"............138
Mango "Cheesecake" 139
Caramelized Pear Cake 140
No Bake Strawberry Cake.............. 141
Apple Strudel Rice Paper Rolls 142
Chocolate Caramel Dipping Sauce.......143
2 Minute Choc Orange Mousse.........144
Festive Ice Cream Log 145

7 Daily Meal Plans.....................148

A WORD FROM ANJA

I have always had a passion for creating delicious food. However, it wasn't until September 2012 when a heart health scare led me to a plant based lifestyle.

This meant re-educating myself about ingredients and finding easy ways of cooking my favorite recipes, using healthy vegan ingredients. I found this challenging, but in a fun way!

New ways of cooking, new ingredients and a whole new range of tastes and flavors that I had never been awake to before - and better yet, I didn't have to include animal products for me to eat well and get all of the nutrients that I need to be healthy :-)

Since then I have lost over 50 pounds (24 kilos) and at 42 I have more energy now than I did when I was 20.

Thanks to inspirational plant based doctors such as T. Colin Campbell, Caldwell Esselstyn, Michael Greger, John McDougall and Neal Barnard, I discovered the science behind eating a whole food plant based diet and that animal proteins and cholesterol are the root of many of our western diseases.

This is such a simple, healthy and energizing way to eat and I hope that you enjoy these recipes as much as I do.

Yours in cooking and eating,
Anja Cass
www.cookingwithplants.com

Breakfast

Coconut Chia Fruit Bowl P20

Two Ingredient Pancakes P19

Savory French Toast P15

DATE BANANA PORRIDGE SMOOTHIE

This is a great porridge on the run for those busy days.

INGREDIENTS

10 whole medjool dates pitted
1 whole banana ripe
½ cup oats
1 tsp vanilla extract
1 litre/1 quart water

SERVINGS: 2

INSTRUCTIONS

1 Put all the ingredients in a blender and blend for approximately 1 minute or until smooth and creamy.

Super fast, healthy, easy and surprisingly filling for a busy morning schedule!

HIGH ENERGY BREAKFAST SMOOTHIE

Kick start your day with this nutrition filled green smoothie!

INGREDIENTS

2 big handfuls spinach leaves
½ whole cantaloupe/rockmelon, peeled and chopped
1 ½ cups red grapes seedless
½ cup ice optional
1 small avocado
3 cups coconut water

SERVINGS: 2

INSTRUCTIONS

1 As this is a smoothie recipe a good blender is a must! Simply put in all the ingredients and blend until you have a nice smooth consistency.

 RECIPE NOTES

For a cool refreshing twist, freeze your grapes before adding to this smoothie.

SOY YOGURT

This soy yogurt is easy to make and doesn't need any special probiotics.

INGREDIENTS

250 grams/8.75 ounces tofu (organic if possible, medium to firm)

2 tbs lemon juice

1 cup soy milk (organic if possible)

½ cup boiling water

10 fresh red chilies (with stems)

 RECIPE NOTES

For a video demonstration of this recipe, visit:

www.cookingwithplants.com/recipe/soy-yogurt-dairy/

SERVINGS: 4

INSTRUCTIONS

1 Wash tofu and pat dry with a tea towel or paper towel.

2 Place tofu in a blender and add freshly squeezed lemon juice.

3 Add soy milk to blender.

4 Add boiling water to blender and blend everything up for about one minute until a creamy consistency.

5 Pour mixture into a bowl.

6 Remove stems from chilies and stand them in the yogurt mixture, making sure the stem base is pushed well into the yogurt mix.

7 Let sit at warm room temperature for about 7 ½ hours or until it has the consistency that you prefer.

8 Remove chili stems and serve with anything you like to add to your yogurt! Enjoy!!

CREAMED VANILLA RICE PUDDING

Simple, filling and tasty. A great eat and run recipe!

INGREDIENTS

4 cups water (or plant milk for extra creaminess)

1 cup rice (I used short grain white)

¼ tsp coarse celtic sea salt

¼ cup sugar, or agave syrup

2 tsp vanilla extract

1 cup plant milk (soy, almond, rice, coconut etc) - add at end

 RECIPE NOTES

TIP: This is great served with Oven Roasted Fruits in Syrup - Page 127.

SERVINGS: 2 - 4

INSTRUCTIONS

1. Add water, rice and salt to a pot and bring to a boil. Stir and turn down the heat to low.

2. Leave on gentle simmer (stirring occasionally) for 20 - 25 minutes or until water is absorbed.

3. Add sugar and keep stirring till mixed through (about 2 minutes).

4. Take off heat.

5. Stir vanilla through. Put a lid on and let sit for 5 minutes.

6. Stir plant milk through and serve warm or put in a bowl and cover with plastic wrap pressed down on the rice to stop the top from going hard.

POLENTA PORRIDGE WITH APRICOT DRIZZLE

If you're cold and hungry, this will hit the spot!

INGREDIENTS

Polenta Porridge

1 cup polenta (medium or coarse ground cornmeal)
2 cups water
2 cup plant milk (+ 1 cup extra for serving)
⅓ cup raisins (or sultanas/ chopped dried fruit)
2 tbs sugar (optional)

Apricot Cinnamon Drizzle

2 tbs thick apricot jam/ fruit conserve
1 tsp vanilla extract (or 1 vanilla pod, scraped)
½ tsp cinnamon, ground
1 - 2 tbs boiled hot water

SERVINGS: 2 - 4

INSTRUCTIONS

1 Combine all of the ingredients in a pot (excluding the extra cup of plant milk).

2 Heat over medium to high heat till gently bubbling. Stir constantly.

3 Lower heat, keep at a simmer and stir until thickened.

Note: If mixture starts to splatter, turn heat off and lift pot up slightly to stop the splatter. Put back down when possible.

4 Once thickened, remove from heat and serve with some of the extra plant milk to add extra creaminess, and top with apricot cinnamon drizzle.

Apricot Cinnamon Drizzle

1 Combine all drizzle ingredients in a small bowl or glass jar and mix together until well combined.

BAKLAVA QUINOA PORRIDGE

An exotic and flavor filled breakfast that will warm you up and put a smile on your face!

INGREDIENTS

Quinoa Porridge

1 cup quinoa, rinsed and drained

1 cup water

1 cup plant milk (almond/soy/rice/oat etc)

+ 1 cup extra for serving

2 large pieces of lemon peel

1 tsp vanilla extract

¼ cup apple puree

pinch of salt (coarse celtic sea salt), optional

Baklava Topping:

2 tbs coconut sugar

1 tsp ground cinnamon

¼ cup pistachios

2 tbs walnuts

SERVINGS: 2 - 4

INSTRUCTIONS

Quinoa Porridge

1 Add all ingredients (except extra plant milk) to a pot.

2 Bring to full boil and continue to boil for 1 minute. Stir. Turn heat off.

3 Put lid on pot and let sit on hot stove/burner for 20 minutes. The residual heat will continue to cook the quinoa.

4 Remove the lemon peel and serve warm or cold and top with extra plant milk and baklava topping.

Baklava Topping

1 Pulse in a coffee grinder, blender or small food processor.

 RECIPE NOTES

Tip: Optional Extra Toppings such as maple syrup and coconut cream are delicious!

Tip: Use coconut milk as your plant milk for an extra creamy breakfast.

NO COOK BUCKWHEAT PORRIDGE

A great alternative to the usual oatmeal, and gluten free!

INGREDIENTS

⅓ cup buckwheat
1 cup water
1 cup plant milk (soy, almond, rice, coconut)
1 large ripe banana

Topping Suggestions:
Nuts, seeds, shredded coconut, maple syrup, sliced fruit, dried fruit, frozen berries, chia gel, extra buckwheat from reserved.

SERVINGS: 1 - 2

INSTRUCTIONS

1 Place buckwheat in a bowl and soak in water for a minimum of 20 minutes.

2 Place into a strainer and rinse. Keep one tablespoon of the mixture aside in a small container for serving later.

3 Place rest of the mixture in a blender with plant milk and banana.

4 Put into a bowl and top with reserved buckwheat mixture and whatever toppings you like.

SWEET FRENCH TOAST

Decadent, Delicious and Delightful!

INGREDIENTS

2 slices toast bread

Batter:
⅛ cup chickpea flour
(besan flour)
½ tsp cinnamon
1 tsp vanilla extract
1 tsp coconut sugar
⅓ cup plant milk (soy,
almond, rice, coconut etc)

Topping Suggestions:
Banana, apple slices,
pears, dried fruit, frozen
berries, dried coconut,
maple syrup, extra
cinnamon, extra coconut
sugar, chopped nuts,
coconut cream etc

SERVINGS: 2

INSTRUCTIONS

1 Cut each slice of bread into 3 pieces.

2 Mix dry ingredients together in a bowl.

3 Add plant milk and mix until well combined.

4 Coat each piece of bread in batter and put in a hot non-stick frying pan over medium to high heat.

5 Cook on both sides till lightly crisped.

Note: sprinkle a bit of extra sugar before flipping..

SAVORY FRENCH TOAST

OMG! This is the BEST Savory French toast ever... I have just blown my own mind!

INGREDIENTS

4 slices toast bread

Batter:
⅔ cup chickpea flour (besan flour))
1 tsp coarse celtic sea salt
¼ tsp white pepper
⅓ cup nutritional yeast
2 tsp dried basil
⅔ cup plant milk (soy, almond, rice)

Topping Suggestions:
Hummus, chickpeas, avocado, tomato, mushrooms, spinach etc

SERVINGS: 4 SLICES

INSTRUCTIONS

1 Mix dry ingredients together in a bowl.

2 Add plant milk and mix until well combined.

3 Coat bread in batter and put in a hot non-stick frying pan over medium to high heat.

4 Cook on both sides till lightly crisped.

 RECIPE NOTES

TIP: You could place these in the oven to stay warm.

Also, ⅔ cup plant milk makes a lovely thick coating for the toast. Use 1 cup plant milk for a thinner coating if you want a lighter toast coating or you have more bread to coat. I prefer the thicker coating myself!

TOFU SCRAMBLE

This is a super easy vegan tofu scramble recipe that only takes minutes to make and tastes delicious.

INGREDIENTS

500 grams/17.5 ounces firm tofu (washed)

3 tbs nutritional yeast

1 tsp garlic powder

1 tsp onion powder

¼ tsp turmeric

2 tsp chives dried or fresh

2 tsp mixed Italian herbs (dried)

1 tbs tamari (or soy sauce/ Braggs aminos)

1 tsp chili flakes, dried (optional)

¼ tsp himalayan black salt (optional, but gives an egg-like flavor)

½ tsp white pepper

You can also add any other spices, herbs or vegetables that you like e.g. mushrooms, onions, garlic, steamed broccoli etc.

 RECIPE NOTES

Serve the scramble with a side of whole wheat or gluten free toast and garnish with fresh tomato, herbs (I like chives, fresh coriander) and even some fresh chili if you like spice!

SERVINGS: 2 - 3

INSTRUCTIONS

1 Firstly you will need a large frying pan. Stainless steel or non-stick both work well.

2 Crumble up the tofu into small pieces so it takes on the look of scrambled eggs.

3 Add all the other ingredients into the mix.

4 Set your cook top to high and place the fry pan on the heat.

5 Put aside about half a cup of water next to the fry pan, you will need it as the tofu begins to stick to the pan.

6 Stirring regularly, cook the scramble thoroughly and add little amounts of water to stop the scramble from sticking, or to give it a softer texture.

7 After about 5 minutes the tofu should be cooked and heated through. Use your own judgment as to when it's ready to eat.

BREAKFAST COUSCOUS BITES

Tasty on their own, even better on toast with caramelized onion and avocado!

INGREDIENTS

Dry Ingredients:

1 cup uncooked couscous
3 tbs whole wheat flour
2 tbs chickpea flour (besan flour)
2 tsp coarse celtic sea salt
⅛ tsp white pepper
2 tsp smoked paprika
½ tsp onion powder
½ tsp garlic powder
1 tsp fennel seeds
¼ tsp ground sage
1 tsp mixed Italian herbs

Wet Ingredients:

1 cup hot boiled water

SERVINGS: 8 BITES

INSTRUCTIONS

1 Stir all of the dry ingredients together in a bowl until well combined.

2 Add hot water, stir and mix well.

3 Let sit for 5 minutes and allow mixture to firm up and cool down.

4 Shape into 8 bites.

5 Heat a non-stick pan and cook a minute or two on each side until heated through.

6 OR, bake in oven at 180°C/360°F for 15 to 20 minutes, turning half way through.

TWO INGREDIENT WAFFLES

Cheap and easy waffles for any time of day!

INGREDIENTS

3 cups oats
1 ripe banana
2 ½ cups water

SERVINGS: 8 WAFFLES

INSTRUCTIONS

1 All you need for this recipe is a blender and a waffle iron.

2 First, turn on the waffle iron to get it hot.

3 Put all the ingredients in a blender and blend until smooth - about 1 minute

4 If your waffle iron is non stick you can pour the mixture straight in without oil.

5 Cook for approximately 5 minutes until you have a golden brown waffle!

6 Repeat until full!

TWO INGREDIENT PANCAKES

A fool-proof super easy pancake recipe without oil, eggs or dairy!

INGREDIENTS

⅔ cup chick pea flour (besan flour)

1 whole banana ripe

½ cup water + a little extra water if the batter thickens too much

SERVINGS: 2 - 4

INSTRUCTIONS

1 For this recipe you will need a blender and ideally a quality non-stick pan.

2 First, get your pan onto the stove and set the heat to medium.

3 Now add all the ingredients into your blender and blend for approximately 1 minute until the batter is nice and smooth.

4 Now it's simply a matter of cooking the pancakes till golden brown.

5 Serve with your favorite toppings.

COCONUT CHIA FRUIT BOWL

Filling, yet light and healthy!

INGREDIENTS

¼ cup chia seeds

1 ¼ cups coconut milk (or plant milk of choice)

1 tsp vanilla extract

Topping Suggestions:
Fresh fruit, shredded coconut, maple syrup, coconut sugar.

 RECIPE NOTES

TIP: For a lighter version use lite soy milk and a dash of coconut essence.

SERVINGS: 2

INSTRUCTIONS

1 Put all of the ingredients in a screw top jar and shake well.

2 Let sit for 5 minutes and shake again.

3 Wait 10 minutes till thick or leave in refrigerator overnight for really thick version (easy to keep on hand).

4 Top with your favorite fruit and shredded coconut.

"EGGY" BREAKFAST MUFFINS

If you miss your eggs, give this one a go!

INGREDIENTS

170 grams/6 ounces firm tofu (organic if possible)

⅓ cup soy milk

1 tsp dijon mustard

1 small clove garlic

1 tbs chickpea flour (besan flour)

1 tbs corn starch (or arrowroot powder)

1 tsp dried herbs

⅛ tsp turmeric (for color only)

½ tsp Himalayan black salt (optional, but does give an egg-like taste)

¼ tsp coarse celtic sea salt

Topping Suggestions:

Black pepper, chili flakes, sliced green onions, fresh herbs.

SERVINGS: 3 - 4 MUFFINS

INSTRUCTIONS

1 Preheat oven to 175°C/350°F.

2 Remove tofu from packet and rinse under water. Pat dry and add to blender.

3 Add all remaining ingredients to the blender and blend until smooth.

Note: The texture will be quite thick like mayonnaise.

4 Scoop mixture into a lightly oiled non-stick muffin pan or lined muffin cups until all batter is used.

Note: fills about 3 to 4 muffin holes to the brim.

5 Bake for 20 minutes. Check muffins with a skewer or toothpick. If it comes out clean, it has cooked right through.

6 Let the muffins sit at room temperature for at least 10 minutes, then carefully remove them from the muffin tray.

7 Serve and enjoy!

POTATO HASH BROWNS

A fantastic healthy potato snack that tastes like it should be bad!

INGREDIENTS

1 large potato peeled, washed and patted dry.
2 tbs brown rice flour
¼ tsp coarse Celtic sea salt
1 pinch white pepper

SERVINGS: 4

INSTRUCTIONS

1 All you need for this recipe is a mixing bowl and a non stick frying pan.

2 First of all, grate your potato into a heat proof mixing bowl. Then microwave it for one and a half minutes on full power. (My microwave is 1100W).

Note: If you do not like or have a microwave you could steam your potato in a bowl for a few minutes to soften it.

3 Once the potato is soft, mix in the rest of the ingredients into the bowl with a fork.

4 Next, separate the mixture into 4 separate portions and get your non stick pan heating up on a low to medium heat.

5 Wetting your hands first, grab a portion of potato and shape it into your favorite hash brown shape before placing it straight into the pan.

6 Cook for approximately 5 minutes per side or until golden brown. Best served straight away!

CHICKPEA OMELETTE

This is the best egg-free and soy free vegan omelette ever!

INGREDIENTS

⅔ cup water

⅓ cup chickpea flour (besan flour)

1 tbs flax seeds (ground)

1 tbs nutritional yeast, optional

⅛ tsp baking powder

¼ tsp Himalayan black salt, optional (adds an egg flavor)

¼ tsp white pepper

¼ tsp turmeric

¼ tsp coarse celtic sea salt

½ tsp garlic powder

⅛ tsp chili flakes, optional

Topping Suggestions:
Mushrooms, spinach, char-grilled red peppers, pesto, hummus, potatoes etc

SERVINGS: 1

INSTRUCTIONS

1 For this recipe it is nice to have a blender, however, you can mix the ingredients manually. You will also need a medium sized non stick pan with a lid (preferably glass so you can see how it is cooking).

2 Place the ingredients into your blender and blend till smooth.

3 Pour the mixture into the pan and place on a low to medium heat. Cover the pan with a lid for 3-4 minutes until the top of the omelette has a sponge-like consistency (quite firm on top like bread).

4 From here you can either fold in your favorite ingredients and serve or turn over the omelette to brown both sides.

HOMEMADE BAKED BEANS

So much tastier than the store bought alternative.

INGREDIENTS

1 400 gram/14 ounce can cannellini beans (including liquid, organic in bpa free can preferred)

1 400g gram/14 ounce can cannellini beans, drained

1 400g gram/14 ounce can crushed tomatoes

1 tbs coconut sugar (or raw cane sugar)

1 ½ tsp coarse celtic sea salt

¼ tsp white pepper

1 tsp smoked paprika

2 tbs cornstarch

1 tbs maple syrup

1 tsp dijon mustard

SERVINGS: 4

INSTRUCTIONS

1 Put everything in a pot and stir through so that the cornstarch is mixed through well.

2 Turn heat on to medium and stir until thickened and warm.

3 Serve warm or let cool. YUM!

ZUCCHINI CORN FRITTERS

Light, savory and awesomely tasty with some cashew cream!

INGREDIENTS

extra large zucchini (375g/12oz)

½ cup whole wheat flour

2 tsp onion flakes

1 tsp coarse celtic sea salt

¼ tsp white pepper

2 tsp mixed Italian herbs, dried

⅓ cup chickpea flour (besan flour)

2 corn cobs, kernels

½ cup water

Chili - optional to taste

SERVINGS: 16 FRITTERS

INSTRUCTIONS

1 Mix all ingredients together (except water) in a bowl.

2 Add water and mix again.

3 Spoon into medium-hot non stick frying pan and cook a few minutes on each side until cooked through.

4 You can place them in the oven to keep warm.

 RECIPE NOTES

TIP: Great served with cashew sour cream - Page 101.

LEMON BLUEBERRY MUFFINS

Great for morning tea, and kids love them.

INGREDIENTS

1 large banana (or 2 small)
3 cups oats
1 cup whole wheat flour
1 tsp baking powder
2 cups water (or plant milk)
½ cup lemon juice
2 tsp vanilla extract
¼ cup sugar, optional
¼ cup poppy seeds
1 cup blueberries

Fruit Jelly Topping:

2 tbs 100% fruit conserve
(jam/jelly - any flavor you
like eg. apricot, blueberry)
1 tbs maple syrup
5 tbs hot boiled water

 RECIPE NOTES

TIP: You can also use this recipe to make pancake fingers! Simply use this mixture and cook them as pancakes. Slice them into thick strips and serve them with fruit jelly topping or maple syrup, extra blueberries and any other toppings you like. eg. nuts, coconut sugar, bananas, coconut cream etc

Makes 15 pancakes!

SERVINGS: 12 - 18 MUFFINS

INSTRUCTIONS

1 Mix all ingredients together in a bowl until just combined.

2 Divide the muffin mixture into 12 or 18 non-stick or paper lined muffin cups.

3 Bake at 175°C/350°F for 25 minutes or until skewer or toothpick comes out clean.

4 Prick holes into the tops of the hot muffin with a skewer or toothpick and pour the fruit jelly mix evenly over each one.

5 Place in oven for another 5 minutes.

6 Take out of oven and let sit for 5 minutes minimum or until muffins are cooled.

Fruit Jelly Topping

1 Mix all ingredients together in a bowl or glass jar until well combined.

ALMOND CHAI LATTE

A super tasty almond chai latte recipe you can make in just minutes at home - this is my favorite!

INGREDIENTS

2 tbs almond butter (almond paste)
2 ½ cups boiled water
1 tbs maple syrup
5 whole medjool dates, pitted
2 tsp cinnamon
2 tsp vanilla extract
¼ tsp coarse celtic sea salt
½ tsp cardamon powder
½ tsp ground ginger
⅛ tsp all spice
¼ tsp nutmeg

 RECIPE NOTES

For a nice finishing touch, I glaze the rim of my glass with some brown rice syrup and then dip it into a mix of coconut sugar and cinnamon. This makes it look great and taste even better!

SERVINGS: 2

INSTRUCTIONS

1 All you need for this simple recipe is a blender and a kettle!

2 First up, make sure your kettle has at least 3 cups of water in it and set to boil.

3 Once the kettle has boiled, place all the ingredients into your blender.

4 You will need to blend the ingredients for 1 - 2 minutes until nice and creamy.

Important: Be careful when blending a hot drink. Make sure that the top of your blender is not completely sealed. You do not want pressure to build up in the blender as it can potentially spray hot beverage all over your kitchen!

Main Meals

Pizza in a Pan P30

Vegetable Black Bean Loaf P52

Jackfruit Peri Peri Skewers + Salsa P59

PIZZA IN A PAN

This stovetop pizza is simple, fast and delicious!

INGREDIENTS

2 cups flour (any you like)
1 tsp baking powder
1 tsp dry instant yeast
1 tsp coarse celtic sea salt
1 cup water (you may need to add a little more water to get a very thick batter consistency)

Topping Suggestions:
Tomato paste, hummus, olives, falafels, mushrooms, tomatoes, fresh herbs, spinach, pre-cooked potatoes, red peppers, diced cucumbers, dried herbs etc

 RECIPE NOTES

Tip: This recipe makes a thick crust pizza. If you prefer a thin crust, simply halve the recipe and cook as per instructions for thick crust.

Tip: For gluten free base use 1 cup brown rice flour + 1 cup chickpea flour.

Tip: Great topped with my white sauce from page 102 or cheese sauce from mac and cheese recipe page 33.

SERVINGS: 1 PIZZA

INSTRUCTIONS

1 Place all of the ingredients in a non-stick frying pan (mine is 20cm/11in). Stir gently with a rubber spatula or back of a wooden spoon.

2 Flatten mixture out evenly in the pan to form your pizza base. It will be like a very thick batter.

3 Add toppings, starting with tomato paste.

4 Cover the pan with a lid, making sure that it is tightly closed for 5 minutes on medium to high heat.

5 Open vents or tilt lid slightly so a little bit of air and moisture can escape. Continue to cook on medium for another 15 minutes.

6 Take off heat. Remove lid. Gently remove pizza from pan and serve hot. I like to serve on a wooden board as it helps keep the base nice and crispy.

NO KNEAD PIZZA

This is the easiest pizza dough recipe ever!

INGREDIENTS

2 cups whole wheat flour

1 cup plain flour (all purpose flour)

1 tsp instant dried yeast

1 tsp coarse celtic sea salt

2 cups water (at room temperature)

1 pinch marjoram (dried)

1 pinch white pepper

Topping Suggestions:

Tomato paste, hummus, olives, falafels, mushrooms, tomatoes, fresh herbs, spinach, pre-cooked potatoes, red peppers, diced cucumbers, dried herbs etc

 RECIPE NOTES

Tip: Serve on a wooden board as it absorbs moisture and keeps the base crispy!

Great topped with white sauce from Page 102 or cheese sauce from mac & cheese recipe Page 33.

INSTRUCTIONS

1 Before you start, you will need a large mixing bowl, wooden spoon, one to two baking trays (preferably pizza trays) lined with non stick parchment paper and a tea towel.

2 First, mix all the dry ingredients in bowl until well combined. Add the water and mix until you have a moist dough that is pulling away from the edge of the bowl.

3 Leave dough in bowl, cover with a tea towel and place in a warm draft free area for approximately 1 hour until the dough has risen and doubled in size.

4 Once the dough has risen, preheat oven to 210°C/420°F. Uncover the dough and separate into two halves with your mixing spoon. Spoon each half onto separate baking trays and spread by hand with slightly wet fingers into the shape of a pizza base.

5 From here on you have two options:

Option 1: Cook the bases for later use or freezing.

First up decide if you want a thin or thick base. If you want a thicker base let the pizza dough sit on the baking tray for 20 minutes in a warm area prior to baking.

If you want thin bases simply pop them in the oven and cook on both sides for 7-10 minutes until lightly browned. (Do not overcook them as they will be baked again with your toppings later).

Option 2: Cook the pizzas now!

If you are busy like me, you can opt to top the pizza dough on the tray and then bake for the whole lot for 15-25 minutes.

GLUTEN FREE QUINOA CRUSTED PIZZA

A gluten free pizza recipe that tastes amazing!

INGREDIENTS

Pizza base

2 ⅔ cups quinoa flour
3 tbs arrowroot
2 tsp instant yeast
1 tsp coarse celtic sea salt
1 cup mashed potato
1 ¼ cup warm water
(I used the starchy water from cooked potatoes)

Cheesy Sauce Ingredients

⅓ cup water
2 tbs nutritional yeast
⅓ cup oats (gluten free variety) or cashews
1 clove garlic
1 tbs miso paste (I use organic brown rice miso)
1 tsp coarse celtic sea salt

SERVINGS: 2 PIZZAS

INSTRUCTIONS

Crusty Pizza Base

1   For this recipe you will need a large bowl, wooden spoon, 2 pizza trays and some non stick parchment paper.

2   Add all the dry ingredients into the mixing bowl and stir to combine.

3   Now add the mash potato and work it through the mixture before adding the starchy warm water.

4   Mix the dough thoroughly by hand, then work into a large ball before covering the mixing bowl with a tea towel for 20 minutes to allow the yeast to do its work!

5   While the dough is proving, get your oven heating up to 220°C/440°F.

6   Once the dough has risen you will see that it feels spongy. Line your pizza trays with non-stick parchment paper. Divide the dough in half, slightly wet your hands and flatten into pizza base shapes on the pizza trays.

7   Bake your pizza bases for 10-20 minutes each side depending on how crispy you like your base. Put favorite toppings on and bake for another 5 to 10 minutes.

Cheesy Sauce

1   Before commencing you will need a small blender and ideally a squeeze bottle to both store the sauce and make it easy to apply to the pizza.

2   Simply pop all the ingredients into your blender and blend for approximately 1 minute or until smooth and creamy.

3   Pour the mixture into your squeeze bottle through a strainer to catch any lumps the blender may have missed.

MAC & "CHEESE"

This vegan mac and cheese has no dairy or oil and tastes better than the traditional version!

INGREDIENTS

500 grams/17.5 ounces macaroni (pre cooked)

2 cups water boiled

2 cups potatoes (diced and boiled or steamed)

1 cup sweet potato (diced and boiled or steamed. you could also use carrot, pumpkin or squash.)

¼ cup oats

¼ cup nutritional yeast

2 tsp coarse celtic sea salt

¼ tsp white pepper

1 tsp onion powder

1 tsp garlic powder

1 tbs lemon juice

1 tbs miso paste

¼ cup pine nuts (optional)

1 tbs tahini (optional)

SERVINGS: 2 - 4

INSTRUCTIONS

1 First up you will need to have your macaroni, potato & sweet potato boiled and ready to go. For the rest of the recipe you will only need a blender.

2 Pop all the ingredients in the blender (except the macaroni).

Note: Feel free to use the hot water from cooking the pasta or potatoes rather than boiling more.

3 If you choose to use the pine nuts and tahini you will get a much creamier sauce but it will be higher in fat and calories.

4 Blend for approximately 1 minute or until smooth.

Important: Before you blend the ingredients make sure you vent the blender slightly or you can build up pressure in the blender resulting in a mac & cheese explosion!

5 Give the mixture a taste test and add extra seasoning if necessary.

6 Finally, simply pour the sauce over your pasta, mix and serve!

POTATO CRUSTED QUICHE

The best tasting eggless quiche ever!
And it looks great on the plate!

INGREDIENTS

The Quiche Crust

2 whole potatoes
(organic if possible, peeled and sliced thinly)

Quiche Filling

1 tbs nutritional yeast
⅓ cup chick pea flour (besan flour)
¼ cup cashews raw
½ cup oats
1 cup plant milk (almond/ soy/rice/oat etc)
3 tbs lemon juice 2-4 cloves garlic
1 tsp coarse celtic sea salt
1 tsp himalayan black salt
(or use another ⅓ tsp of coarse celtic sea salt)
1 tsp dijon mustard
280 grams/10 ounces artichoke (drained from brine)
2 cups baby spinach leaves

Quiche Dressing

2 cups butternut pumpkin (squash)
(chopped into 1cm (½") chunks and cooked till soft)

SERVINGS: 1 LARGE QUICHE

INSTRUCTIONS

Creating the crust

1. First, you will need a 9.5" or 24cm round pie dish lightly oiled to prevent sticking and a high quality blender/ food processor. Set the oven to 200°C/400°F .

2. Place the potato slices around the base to make the crust.

3. Place the pie dish in the oven for approximately 10 minutes until the potato edges are starting to brown and the flesh has softened.

The Quiche Filling

1. While the crust is cooking place all the filling ingredients except the artichokes, spinach and pumpkin in your blender/processor and blend until smooth and creamy.

2. Now add the spinach and artichoke and pulse the blender/processor until they are coarsely chopped.

Making the Quiche

1. Once the crust is ready, take it out of the oven and onto your bench top. Pour the quiche filling into the dish leaving approximately 2cm (3/4") at the top, then smooth the mixture out nice and evenly.

2. Pour the steamed pumpkin over the top of the mixture and gently work the pieces in, making sure some of the pumpkin is left exposed so it looks better when served.

3. Sprinkle the top of the quiche with your favorite seasoning. I used nutmeg and pepper!

4. Finally, place the quiche dish back in the oven at the same temperature for approximately 30 minutes or until cooked through.

5. Once cooked, set the quiche out on a bench to cool for at least 5-10 minutes so it can firm up.

6. Serve the quiche hot or cold with your favorite sides. I like a nice garden salad with a little balsamic vinegar!

MEDITERRANEAN POLENTA STACKS

Fast, easy and totally delicious polenta recipe that looks great and tastes out of this world!

INGREDIENTS

Polenta Bases

½ cup polenta (medium/coarse cornmeal)

1½ cups water

3 tbs nutritional yeast

1 tsp garlic powder

1 tsp onion powder

1 tsp coarse celtic sea salt

¼ tsp white pepper

2 tbs hummus (or tahini)

Topping Ingredients

2 whole roasted red peppers (capsicums) pickled from a store bought jar cut into thin strips

1 whole avocado ripe

½ cup tomato roma - finely chopped

¼ cup onion Spanish - finely chopped

3 sprigs cilantro, whole (or fresh herbs of choice)

2 cloves garlic finely chopped

½ tsp coarse celtic sea salt

1 whole lime, juiced

SERVINGS: 3

INSTRUCTIONS

1 First up you will need a large pot and stirring spoon.

2 Add all the polenta ingredients to your pot and apply high heat while stirring briskly.

3 Once the mixture reaches boiling point, turn the heat down and keep stirring until you have a nice thick mash potato consistency.

4 Take the pot off the heat and start to spoon the mixture into your chosen molds. For my molds I used mini spring form cake tins and made the Polenta about 1/2 inch(12mm) high.

5 Place the molds in the refrigerator for approximately 5 minutes to set.

TOPPING INSTRUCTIONS

1 While the Polenta sets scoop out the avocado into a bowl.

2 Add garlic, salt and lime then use a fork to blend the mixture into a chunky guacamole consistency.

3 Take the polenta molds out of the refrigerator, remove the polenta base and place on a plate, and commence stack building!

4 I suggest starting with the capsicum, followed by the guacamole, onion, tomato and lastly a nice sprig off fresh cilantro or herbs of choice.

5 Add a little balsamic vinegar, chili sauce or similar!

CREAMY POTATO BROCCOLI BAKE

A filling winter favorite!

INGREDIENTS

180 grams/6 ounces broccoli, lightly steamed

5 large potatoes (sliced lengthways and lightly steamed/boiled or microwaved)

2 tbs Italian dried herbs

Paprika or nutmeg for sprinkling over the top

Sauce:

400 gram/14 ounce can cannellini beans, drained

3 cups plant milk (eg. soy, almond, rice milk)

4 tbs cornstarch

1 tsp coarse celtic sea salt

¼ tsp white pepper

1 tbs tahini

1 tbs miso paste

1 tbs nutritional yeast, optional

SERVINGS: 4 - 6

INSTRUCTIONS

1 Start by making the sauce. Blend all of the ingredients and then heat in a pot over high heat.

2 Bring to the boil and lower heat to simmer until thickened. Be sure to stir constantly to avoid the sauce from sticking. Remove from heat and set aside.

3 Get an oven proof baking dish and layer half of the potato, broccoli, dried herbs and sauce. Then do another layer and finish with the sauce. Sprinkle with paprika or nutmeg.

4 Cover with aluminum foil or a lid and bake at 180°C/360°F for 20 minutes.

5 Remove aluminum foil and bake for another 10 to 15 minutes at the same temperature.

RECIPE NOTES

TIP: Serve with a big salad and some crusty bread!

HOMEMADE GNOCCHI

Classic Italian food done Vegan style.

INGREDIENTS

3 tbs water

2 tbs chickpea flour (besan flour)

8 medium potatoes, boiled, peeled and mashed

1 ½ cups whole wheat flour + extra for dusting your hands and work surface

2 tsp coarse celtic sea salt, or to taste

⅛ tsp ground black pepper

 RECIPE NOTES

Tip: Don't cook too many of the gnocchi pieces at once so they cook evenly. Try serving with my pesto sauce page 96 or white sauce page 102... or sauce of your choice!

SERVINGS: 4 - 6

INSTRUCTIONS

1 Combine the water and chickpea flour in a small bowl or jar and mix into a slurry.

2 In a large mixing bowl combine the mashed potatoes and flour. Add the chickpea slurry, salt and pepper and combine well. Knead into a large ball and add a little bit more flour if it is too wet and sticky.

3 Now you are ready to shape your gnocchi. Dust your hands lightly with some flour. Pull off walnut size pieces of dough and run over the prongs of a fork or use a gnocchi board if you have one to shape them into more authentic looking pieces.

4 Put on a floured board or parchment paper until all the dough has been shaped.

5 Bring a large pot of water to boil and drop in gnocchi pieces. They will rise to the top once cooked.

6 Remove with a slotted spoon and serve.

SWEET POTATO FALAFEL BURGERS

Iron & Protein rich with a delicious flavor!

INGREDIENTS

250 grams/8.75 ounces sweet potato - boiled, drained and dry mashed

2 cups canned chickpeas, drained

⅓ cup chickpea flour (besan flour)

2 tbs dried basil

1 tsp smoked paprika

½ tsp coarse celtic sea salt, or to taste

¼ tsp white pepper

1 tbs nutritional yeast, optional

1 tsp chili flakes, optional

8 whole wheat bread rolls

Topping Suggestions:
Avocado, lettuce, tomato, onion, pickles

SERVINGS: 4 (8 PATTIES)

INSTRUCTIONS

1 Place all of the ingredients (except bread rolls) into a food processor and process until well combined.

2 Shape into 8 patties and put on a baking tray lined with non-stick parchment paper.

3 Bake in oven at 175°C/350°F for 15 minutes, turn the patties over and bake for an extra 10 to 15 minutes.

4 Remove from oven and allow burgers to cool on the baking tray till they firm up.

5 Serve with your favorite toppings and condiments.

RECIPE NOTES

Tip: Refer to the condiments section of this cookbook for ideas on what you could have on your burgers.

HEARTY MUSHROOM LENTIL BURGERS

Hearty, filling and delicious without the cholesterol!

INGREDIENTS

4 cups mushrooms sliced

400 grams/14 ounces can brown lentils, drained

2 tbs tapioca flour

¼ cup oats

1 tsp onion powder

1 tsp garlic powder

1 tsp fennel seeds whole

1 tbs mixed Italian herbs

1 tsp sage (ground)

1 tsp paprika

1 tbs tomato paste

1 tsp coarse celtic sea salt (to taste)

¼ tsp white pepper

 RECIPE NOTES

Some quick ideas for condiments you could try are vegan mayo, ketchup, mustard, salsa, pickles, chutney....the list is endless!

SERVINGS: 4

INSTRUCTIONS

1   To get started you will need a large frying pan and a food processor. You will also need a large baking tray lined with non-stick parchment paper and an oven running at approximately 200°C/400°F.

2   Place all the chopped mushrooms in the frying pan without water or oil on high heat.

The moisture of the mushrooms will release as they heat up lubricating the pan.

Once cooked, take the mushrooms off the heat and pour them into your food processor.

3   Add the rest of the ingredients into the processor and pulse the mixture 10-15 times before opening and pushing any unprocessed ingredients off the sides. Give the mixture another 5+ pulses until the mixture feels right for making patties.

4   Now it's time to take your lined baking tray and form up approximately 6 patties.

Tip: I used an ice cream scoop to get an even amount of mixture.

5   Pop the patties into the oven for 15 minutes, then turn them over and give them another 10 minutes.

6   While you are waiting for the patties to cook take that time to prepare your rolls, chop some lettuce, tomato, (beetroot if Australian), onions, avocado etc so that you are ready to eat once the patties are cooked!

LASAGNE ROLL UP BAKE

Rich and flavorsome, as any Lasagne recipe should be!

INGREDIENTS

8 lasagne sheets, cooked till soft as per packet instructions

Almond Ricotta:
1 cup almonds
½ cup water
1 tbs chopped scallions
1 tsp coarse celtic sea salt

Vegetable Mince:
1 head cauliflower, pulsed up in food processor (or chopped very small like rice)
¼ cup walnuts, pulsed up in food processor (or chopped very small like rice)
¼ cup salsa (or tinned tomatoes)
1 tsp smoked paprika
2 tsp dried basil
1 tsp dried onion flakes
Salt and pepper to taste

Zucchini Mix:
2 large zucchini, julienned
2 large kale leaves, stalks removed and sliced
½ cup scallions, sliced
1 - 2 tbs vegetable stock
Salt and pepper to taste

Sauce:
1 cup cashews
½ cup pinenuts (or just use more cashews)
1 ½ tsp coarse celtic sea salt
1 ½ cups plant milk (soy/rice/almond/oat)
3 tbs lemon juice
3 tbs tapioca starch

INSTRUCTIONS

Almond Ricotta

1. Blend until combined and still a little bit chunky.

Vegetable Mince

1. Cook over high heat in a non-stick fry pan until well browned and quite dry (or use ground "meat" recipe on **page 47**)

Zucchini Mix

1. Cook over high heat in a non-stick fry pan just until zucchini and kale have softened.

Sauce

1. Put all ingredients in a blender and blend till smooth.

Assembly

1. Place the lasagne sheets on some non-stick parchment paper in a single layer.

2. Spread the Ricotta over the top of each piece. Then spread the Vegetable Mince on top.

3. Next, place the zucchini mix on top and season to taste. Roll up and place into a large baking dish or two small baking dishes of your choice.

4. Evenly pour the sauce over the top, sprinkle with paprika or nutmeg if you wish and bake in the oven at 180°C/360°F for 30 minutes or until the top is fluffy and lightly browned.

CABBAGE TERRINE

Great color and a fresh summer taste!

INGREDIENTS

8 -10 large cabbage leaves (blanched in hot boiling water for 1 minute)

1 sweet potato - cooked, cooled and sliced

5 large potatoes - cooked, cooled and sliced

2 large sliced red bell peppers
 (grilled and pickled in a jar, store-bought is fine)

1 large kale leaf, stalk removed

2 cloves garlic, sliced

1 onion, peeled and sliced lengthways

2 tsp smoked paprika, or to taste

Salt and pepper to taste

Wedges of lemon for serving, optional

 RECIPE NOTES

Tip: This also tastes great with layers of pesto as per recipe on page 96 and Cashew Sour Cream page 101 on top.

SERVINGS: 4 - 6

INSTRUCTIONS

1   Cook the kale, garlic and onion in a non-stick fry pan until the onions are golden. Use a tablespoon or two of water if they start to stick. Set aside.

2   Line a bread tin with some non-stick parchment paper.

3   Carefully place the cabbage leaves across the bread tin so they cover the bottom and sides of the container. Extra cabbage will hang over the edges at this point and this will be folded over at the end to encase the entire terrine.

4   Next, place one layer of potatoes in the bottom. Then place all of the grilled peppers on top. Spread evenly and be sure that you keep putting light pressure on all the layers as you put them in so the terrine stays firm and holds together.

5   Put a dash of salt and pepper and put another layer of potato. Sprinkle with some smoked paprika.

6   Next, add the kale mix and spread evenly. Then layer on the sweet potato and salt and pepper.

7   Finally top this off with a layer of potato.

8   Fold over the cabbage leaves to enclose the terrine.

9   You can either serve this hot or hold. For cold, place in refrigerator for a few hours to cool.

Alternatively you can place it in a moderate hot oven for 20 minutes until heated through.

10   Slice and serve with a wedge of lemon.

SPICED PUMPKIN SOUP + CASHEW CREAM

A perfect winter dish ideal for feeding hungry visitors!

INGREDIENTS

Pumpkin Soup

900 grams/2 pounds pumpkin or squash, cubed
1 whole onion large, roughly chopped
1 tbs ginger grated
2 whole potatoes large, cubed
¼ tsp nutmeg ground
¼ tsp turmeric ground
¼ tsp white pepper ground
1 litre/1 quart vegetable stock, reduced salt is best
1 tsp coarse celtic sea salt

Cinnamon Cashew Cream

2 cups cashews raw unsalted (soaked in 2 cups of water for at least 1/2 - 1 hour)
1 tsp cinnamon ground
1 tbs maple syrup (pure is best)
1 tsp coarse celtic sea salt

SERVINGS: 6

INSTRUCTIONS

Pumpkin Soup

1. First of all you will need a large pot and stirring spoon.

2. Add all ingredients to the pot and stir prior to heating.

3. Put the pot onto your stove at a high heat and bring to the boil. Once boiling, put on a lid and lower the heat to a simmer for approximately 20 minutes.

4. While you're waiting for the soup to cook it's time to make the cinnamon cream! See below.

5. Once the 20 minutes is up and the potato and pumpkin are soft, take the soup off the stove.

6. Add one cup of your freshly made cinnamon cream to the soup and then blend the soup till smooth with either a hand blender, food processor etc. Just be careful if using a hand blender not to spray yourself with hot soup!

Note: Can be blended once cold.

7. Serve the soup in a nice big bowl and dress with an extra swirl of cinnamon cream, sprinkle of nutmeg and some pumpkin seeds for crunch. Now that's Thanksgivinglicious!

Cashew Cream

1. All you need equipment wise for this recipe is a large blender.

2. Place all the ingredients in your blender (including cashew soaking water) and blend for about 1 minute or until smooth and creamy.

BLEND, HEAT & EAT TOMATO SOUP

Really fast, really tasty, really Yum...
...and you can freeze it too!

INGREDIENTS

4 whole tomatoes (riper the better)

2 tbs tomato paste (100% organic is best)

2 cloves garlic (large)

2 tsp oregano (dried or fresh)

1 tsp coconut sugar

¼ tsp cinnamon ground

1 tsp onion powder

½ tsp white pepper

½ tsp coarse celtic sea salt

2 cups vegetable stock

SERVINGS: 2

INSTRUCTIONS

1 For this recipe you will need a blender, large saucepan and stirring ladle or similar.

2 Remove any hard centers from the tomatoes and place all ingredients in the blender.

3 Blend everything for approximately 2 minutes or until smooth.

4 Add mixture to saucepan and apply high heat.

Note: You may find the mixture starts out a little foamy due to the blending process, however, the mixture will settle down during the cooking process.

5 Once the mixture is boiling, drop the heat to a low simmer and place a lid on the saucepan.

6 After approximately 10 minutes you should have a nice rich red tomato soup.

7 Garnish the soup with some fresh Coriander/cilantro and serve with some fresh bread and/or a fresh garden salad - Yum!!

SMOKY LEEK & POTATO SOUP

A great winter dish that keeps well in the refrigerator

INGREDIENTS

2 large leeks, washed and sliced

1 medium onion, chopped

⅛ cup vegetable stock (low sodium)

11 medium potatoes, chopped

1 bunch parsley, roughly chopped

½ tsp coarse celtic sea salt

½ tsp white pepper

¼ cup nutritional yeast

2 tbs lemon juice

3 cups boiling water

2 tbs tamari (or soy sauce/Braggs aminos)

2 tsp liquid smoke, optional but makes it awesome

SERVINGS: 6

INSTRUCTIONS

1 Have all of your vegetables washed, chopped and ready to go!

2 Add leeks, onion and vegetable stock to a large pot and steam fry over medium-high heat for about 5 minutes until vegetables start to soften and release their juices.

3 Add all remaining ingredients except for the Tamari and Liquid Smoke.

4 Stir through, put lid on and simmer on low-medium for 30 to 45 minutes until the potatoes are soft.

5 Add the Tamari and stir through.

6 Remove pot from heat and blend with a hand blender until smooth and creamy.

Note: You can also use a blender or food processor, blend in batches and return to pot.

7 Stir through the liquid smoke.

8 Serve in bowls and garnish as you like. I used parsley and cashew sour cream for this batch!

CREAMY PUMPKIN MINT PEA RISOTTO

Such a filling dish with a delightful blend of flavors!

INGREDIENTS

⅓ large onion, diced (+ water for frying)
1 cup frozen peas
1 cup aborio rice, uncooked
5 cups vegetable stock

Pumpkin Puree:

1 cup steamed or roasted pumpkin
1 cup plant milk (soy/almond/oat/rice)

Add Ins:

2 tbs nutritional yeast, optional
1 tsp coarse celtic sea salt, optional to taste
¼ tsp white pepper
½ to 1 handful of fresh mint leaves, sliced
2 tbs lemon juice

Almond Parmesan:

1 tbs nutritional yeast
¼ cup almonds
1 tsp coarse celtic sea salt

SERVINGS: 2 - 4

INSTRUCTIONS

1 Before you start, prepare your almond parmesan. Add all of the almond parmesan ingredients into a small blender, coffee grinder or small food processor and pulse until ground up. Set aside.

2 Place onion into a non-stick frying pan over high heat. Stir until it starts to brown. Add a tablespoon or two of water to stop the onion from sticking until it turns golden.

3 Add peas to the pan and stir for another 2 minutes.

4 Add rice to the pan and stir for another 3 minutes until the rice gets a little bit toasted.

5 Add the vegetable stock and stir through for a couple of minutes until boiling. Reduce the heat to low and simmer with the lid on for 10 minutes (stir every now and then).

6 In the meantime, blend or puree the pumpkin and plant milk and set aside.

7 Turn rice off and let sit on hot plate (with residual heat) with lid on for 20 to 30 minutes.

8 Add the puree and add ins when ready to serve. Stir through and heat again on medium high heat for a couple of minutes if needed.

9 Top with a sprinkling of almond parmesan. Yum!

LASAGNE STYLE POTATO BAKE

This is a nice hearty dish that both kids and adults love.

INGREDIENTS

5 whole potatoes (boiled, peeled and sliced)

2 small onions (finely diced)

2 cloves garlic (minced)

2 tbs dried herbs (I used parsley, basil, marjoram and sage)

1 medium carrot, grated

2 tsp smoked paprika

½ tsp white pepper

1 tsp cumin seeds

1 tsp chili flakes, optional

2 tbs tomato paste

400 grams/14 ounces chopped tomatoes, canned

1 batch cheese sauce (recipe page 76)

1 batch vegan ground "beef" (recipe page 47)

INSTRUCTIONS

1. For this recipe you will need to make my vegan **Cheese sauce** and my **Vegan Ground Beef** recipes prior to proceeding.

2. Before commencing with this recipe you will need a non stick frying pan, wooden spoon and an 8" × 8" (20 × 20cm) glass baking dish.

3. First add the onion and garlic to your pan and apply a low to medium heat. Use some of the liquid from your canned tomatoes if needed to stop the onions sticking.

4. Once the onions are lightly browned add the carrots and fry for a couple of minutes.

5. Now add all the tomato paste, herbs and spices and take the pan off the stove. Mix thoroughly.

6. Finally, add the vegan ground beef from my prior recipe and mix through. It's now time to get your oven pre-heating to 175°C/350°F.

7. Take your glass baking tray and begin by lining it with a layer of sliced potatoes followed by the vegan "beef" mixture and then a generous layer of vegan cheese sauce.

8. Repeat until the baking dish is full and finish with cheese sauce and a sprinkle of paprika or nutmeg.

9. Bake for 20 minutes or until the vegan cheese has thickened and browned off nicely.

10. Serve with your favorite salad, vegetables and maybe some fresh bread. I am getting hungry!!

VEGAN GROUND "BEEF"

A meat substitute that you can use as taco grounds, pizza topping, bolognese sauce etc.

INGREDIENTS

750g/26 oz cauliflower (1 medium sized cauliflower chopped into large chunks, including core)

1 cup walnuts (100g/3.5oz)

140 grams/5 ounces tomato paste

1 tbs tamari (or soy sauce/ Braggs aminos)

1 tsp smoked paprika

1 tsp coarse celtic sea salt (or to your taste)

⅛ tsp white pepper (or to your taste)

¼ tsp chili flakes

 RECIPE NOTES

You can cook this much quicker if you spread the mixture over a couple of trays rather than just one. Adjust according to your oven settings and quantity being made.

SERVINGS: 6 - 10

INSTRUCTIONS

1 To get started with this recipe you will need either a food processor or good chopping knife and board. You will also need a mixing spoon and a baking tray lined with non-stick parchment paper.

2 Put all the ingredients into the food processor and pulse to a coarse blend (or chop finely by hand).

3 Turn your oven on to 175°C/350°F to preheat, then get your lined baking tray and spread the mixture evenly over the tray.

4 Pop the mixture in the oven for 30 minutes, then take it out and stir the mixture before baking again for another 15 minutes.

Take it out and check again. In my case it needed a further 10 minutes before the crumble was cooked through and the mixture was dry enough.

5 Once cooked you can now store this crumble in the refrigerator ready to make pasta sauces, lasagne, taco meat, pizza toppings and much more! So easy and so delicious!

SHEPHERD'S PIE

A timeless classic done with a vegan twist.

INGREDIENTS

2 carrots, finely diced

1 large onion, diced

2 large portobello mushrooms, diced

2 cups dried french puy lentils (375g/13oz)

1 cup frozen peas

1 sprig of fresh thyme, or ½ tsp dried

1 tbs tomato paste

1 tbs tamari (or soy sauce/ Braggs aminos)

1 tbs balsamic vinegar

3 cups vegetable stock, divided

Salt and pepper to taste

Topping

4 cups mashed potatoes (firm)

 RECIPE NOTES

The mixture should be fairly dry. If it is too runny, thicken with a little bit of cornstarch or rice flour. Cook in individual ramekins for individual serves. Also really tasty topped with almond parmesan recipe on page 95.

SERVINGS: 6 - 8

INSTRUCTIONS

1 Put a pot on medium to high heat and dry fry the carrots until they have softened. Add onion and mushrooms and stir through for a minute or so.

2 Add 1 cup of the stock, soy sauce, balsamic and tomato paste.

3 Stir well and add thyme, peas and lentils.

4 Add another 2 cups of stock and stir through.

5 Lower the heat and simmer without lid for 30 to 40 minutes or until the lentils are tender. Stir occasionally.

6 Take off heat and remove thyme sprig and season with salt and pepper.

7 Put into an 8 × 8 inch (20 × 20 cm) or 5 inch (24cm) pie dish. Top with mashed potato. Scape potato with a fork to roughen the edges - this will make the topping crispier and super delicious.

8 Bake in oven at 180°C/360°F for 30 minutes or until the top is slightly browned and crispy.

STUFFED MUSHROOMS

Perfect for dinner parties

INGREDIENTS

6 large portobello mushrooms

2 tbs sliced scallions

⅛ tbs nutritional yeast

2 tbs chickpea flour (besan flour)

3 tbs cashews

3 tbs oats

⅛ cup plant milk (soy/almond/oat/rice)

1 tbs lemon juice or white vinegar

1 clove garlic

¼ tsp dijon mustard

½ tsp coarse celtic sea salt

 RECIPE NOTES

You can also fill the mushrooms with the risotto from page 45 or the eggplant bolognese on page 51.

SERVINGS: 6 MUSHROOMS

INSTRUCTIONS

1 Carefully remove the stems from the mushrooms and set the mushroom cups aside on a baking tray lined with non-stick parchment paper.

2 Chop up the mushroom stems and stir fry these with the scallions in a non-stick pan. Use a little dash of water if you need to stop them from sticking to the pan. Put this mixture in a small mixing bowl.

3 Place the remaining ingredients in a blender and blend until smooth.

4 Pour the blender mixture into the bowl with the mushroom stems and scallions. Mix well.

5 Evenly distribute the mixture into the mushroom cups.

6 Bake in oven at 180°C/360°F for 20 minutes.

HOMEMADE MARINARA SAUCE

This no oil base recipe is so fresh and full of flavor. Make it your own!

INGREDIENTS

1 kg (2.25lbs) tomatoes, fresh and ripe
1 tsp onion powder
1 tsp dried parsley
1 tsp paprika powder
1 tbs tomato paste
¼ tsp sea salt (celtic or himalayan)
¼ tsp black pepper

 RECIPE NOTES

You can add any extras to this sauce that you like.
e.g. onions, celery, carrot, mushrooms, herbs, and spices. This is a great base sauce and lends itself to a large number of different recipes. Enjoy!

SERVINGS: 4

INSTRUCTIONS

1 Core tomatoes and put a cross slit in the bottom of each one. This will help skins to peel of easily once blanched. Bring a pot of water to the boil and blanch tomatoes for 1 to 2 minutes in the boiling water.

2 Take tomatoes out of hot water with a slotted spoon and place into a bowl of cold water (ice water works best).

3 Remove skins from tomatoes and chop into small cubes.

4 Place tomatoes and remaining ingredients into a pot. Bring to a boil and then reduce heat and simmer for about 15 minutes. You can simmer for longer if you want a thicker sauce.

5 Serve with your favorite pasta, on pizza etc.

EGGPLANT BOLOGNESE

Classic Italian Goodness made healthy!

INGREDIENTS

1 large onion, quartered
2 cloves garlic
4 large tomatoes
1 large eggplant, diced very small
1 large carrot, diced very small or grated
1 large handful fresh basil (with stalks if possible), roughly chopped or sliced
1 tbs paprika
⅓ cup vegetable stock
2 tbs malt vinegar
3 tbs tomato paste Salt and pepper to taste
1 packet of pasta - choose your favorite

SERVINGS: 4

INSTRUCTIONS

1 Before you begin, pulse the onion, garlic and tomatoes in a blender until just combined. Set aside.

2 Heat a non-stick fry pan to medium-high heat. Add eggplant and carrot and stir until vegetables begin to soften.

3 Pour in the blended tomato mixture and keep stirring for a couple of minutes. Add basil and stir through.

4 Next add in the vinegar and tomato paste and stir to mix in. Add the vegetable stock and paprika and stir until the mixture is slightly saucy but not too wet.

5 Remove from heat and add salt and pepper to taste.

6 Serve with your favorite pasta.

VEGETABLE BLACK BEAN LOAF

Great with roast veggies and gravy!

INGREDIENTS

Vegetables:

2 carrots, roughly chopped

1 onion, quartered

3 large portobello mushrooms, quartered (or egg plant/zucchini)

1 large clove garlic, halved

Add Ins:

2 cups black beans, cooked & drained (canned is fine)

1 ½ cups oats

¼ cup tomato paste

1 tsp coarse celtic sea salt

½ tsp ground sage

1 tsp dried basil

2 tsp dried parsley

2 tsp smoked paprika (or regular)

⅛ tsp white pepper

2 tbs nutritional yeast, optional

SERVINGS: 4 - 6

INSTRUCTIONS

1 Steam all of the vegetables until soft.

2 Place steamed vegetables in a food processor and add all of the remaining ingredients.

3 Pulse until well combined but not totally pureed.

4 Pour mixture into a bread loaf pan lined with non-stick parchment paper.

5 Bake in oven at 180°C/360°F for 45 to 60 minutes, or until a skewer or toothpick comes out clean.

6 Let cool for 20 minutes before serving so that it firms up and is easy to slice. Or cool totally and serve cold on sandwiches with the spicy tomato ketchup on **page 109**.

 RECIPE NOTES

Great served with mashed potatoes on page 78 and gravy of your choice from the condiments section of this book.

POTATO & VEGETABLE POLENTA SLICE

Great for a quick meal or when you have guests coming over!

INGREDIENTS

1 cup polenta
3 cups water
¼ cup nutritional yeast
2 tsp garlic powder
2 tsp coarse celtic sea salt
½ tsp white pepper
2 tbs tahini (or hummus)
1 tbs mixed herbs (I used dried basil and parsley)
¼ tsp chili flakes, optional - to taste
2 cups mixed steamed vegetables (chopped into thumb sized pieces)

SERVINGS: 4 - 6

INSTRUCTIONS

1. First up you will need a large sauce pan and stirring spoon.

2. Add all the ingredients (except the vegetables) to your sauce pan and apply medium heat while stirring briskly.

3. Once the mixture reaches a high simmer, turn the heat down and keep stirring until you have a nice thick mash potato consistency and take off heat.

4. Put vegetables into the base of your chosen dish/mold.

5. Spoon the polenta mixture over the vegetables (or mix through). I put mine into a spring-form cake tin lined with nonstick parchment paper.

6. Place in the refrigerator for at least 10 minutes to firm up and set.

STUFFED RED PEPPERS

These taste great with almost any filling!

INGREDIENTS

3 red peppers, cut in half lengthways

1 400g/14oz can diced tomatoes

Stuffing of choice:

Pumpkin Risotto (page 45)

Mac and Cheese (page 33)

Eggplant Bolognese (page 51)

One Pot Mexican Rice (page 58)

Suggested Topping:

Almond Parmesan (page 95)

SERVINGS: 2 - 3

INSTRUCTIONS

1 Put the tin of tomatoes into the base of a baking tray large enough to hold all of the bell pepper halves.

2 Fill each half with the stuffing of your choice and sprinkle with almond parmesan.

3 Bake at 180°C/360°F for 20 minutes, or cook until soft.

 RECIPE NOTES

Steam/Boil/Microwave the peppers slightly first if you prefer very soft peppers. You could also stuff eggplant, mushrooms or zucchini as per this recipe.

CRUMBED "NO FISH" FILLETS

A vegan version of an old classic!

INGREDIENTS

No Fish:

1 tbs flax seeds + 2 tbs water (soaked 5 minutes)

400g/14oz firm organic tofu

1 tbs oats

1 fish sauce recipe (½ cup) (see page 120)

2 tsp coarse celtic sea salt

300g/10.5oz canned green jackfruit, drained

Coating:

1 cup wheat flakes, crushed (or bread crumbs)

⅛ tsp white pepper

½ tbs dried parsley

1 tsp chipotle powder or cajun spice to taste

zest of half a lemon

INSTRUCTIONS

1 Combine all of the coating ingredients on a flat plate and set aside.

2 Combine all of the ingredients for the "no fish" except the jackfruit and place in a food processor. Pulse until smooth. Add the jackfruit and pulse a couple of times until jackfruit resembles chunky "fish" pieces.

3 Shape into 8 or 10 palm sized fillets and crumb both sides with the coating mixture.

4 Place on to a baking tray lined with non-stick parchment paper. Bake at 190°C/380°F for 20 minutes each side or until browned and firm.

RECIPE NOTES

Serve with mayo page 100 or Caesar dressing page 115 and mix through chopped pickles/gherkins.

GREEK STYLE HERBED KOFTAS

The problem with these Koftas is that they always disappear too quickly!

INGREDIENTS

Processor Ingredients

425 gram/15 ounce can chickpeas, drained

1 small handful fresh parsley

1 small handful fresh basil

¼ tsp ground black pepper

⅛ tsp coarse celtic sea salt

1 cup vegetable stock/broth

Mixing Ingredients

1 tbs dried onion flakes

¾ cup gluten flour

⅓ cup chickpea flour (besan flour)

¼ cup nutritional yeast, optional

 RECIPE NOTES

Serve with a big salad, baked potatoes page 79 and cashew sour cream page 101.

SERVINGS: 10 -12 KOFTAS

INSTRUCTIONS

1 Place all of the processor ingredients into a food processor or powerful blender and pulse until moist but slightly chunky.

2 Pour the mixture into a mixing bowl and then add the mixing ingredients. Mix together till well combined.

3 Line a baking tray with some non-stick parchment paper.

4 Divide the mixture into 10 to 12 portions and shape into kofta logs.

5 Cover the tray tightly with aluminium foil and bake in the oven at 180°C/360°F for 30 minutes.

6 Carefully remove the foil, turn the koftas over, and bake for another 15 minutes without foil till browned to your liking.

SUNFLOWER SEED FALAFELS

A modern spin on a traditional favorite

INGREDIENTS

1 cup sunflower seeds, soaked in water at least 2 hours then drained

1 cup broad beans (or fava beans, or chickpeas)

1 large handful cilantro (including stems)

½ handful parsley

½ handful mint leaves

1 tsp coarse celtic sea salt

¼ tsp black pepper

½ tsp chili flakes, optional

2 cloves garlic

2 tbs tahini

1 tsp ground cumin seeds

1 tsp baking soda

SERVINGS: 12 FALAFELS

INSTRUCTIONS

1 Place all of the ingredients in a food processor and process until quite smooth.

2 Divide into 12 portions and shape into small rounds.

3 Place on a baking tray lined with non-stick parchment paper and bake at 180°C/360°F for 20 minutes. Then turn over and bake for another 10 minutes.

 RECIPE NOTES

Serve with Middle Eastern Cauliflower page 83 and Creamy Garlic Sauce page 107.

ONE POT MEXICAN RICE

Lets cross the border into flavor land!

INGREDIENTS

2 cups rice, rinsed

2 cups vegetable stock

1 400g /14oz can diced or crushed tomatoes

1 can beans, drained (eg kidney, cannellini, black)

1 corn cob, kernels

1 tbs tomato paste

1 tbs ground cumin

½ tsp onion powder

1 tsp chili flakes, optional or to taste

½ tsp garlic powder

¼ tsp black pepper, or to taste

½ tsp coarse celtic sea salt

½ tsp dried oregano or basil

SERVINGS: 2 - 4

INSTRUCTIONS

1 Put all of the ingredients in a pot and bring to a boil, stirring. Turn the heat to low and cover with a tight fitting lid. Cook for 13 - 15 minutes.

2 Turn heat off and remove from stove. Let sit, covered, on a bench for 5 minutes.

3 Remove lid. Fluff and serve.

 RECIPE NOTES

Top with sliced avocado and freshly squeezed lime juice.

JACKFRUIT PERI PERI SKEWERS + SALSA

Looks like chicken and tastes great!

INGREDIENTS

200g/7oz green jackfruit - canned, drained, rinsed and cubed

Marinade:

2 tsp tamari (or soy sauce/ Braggs aminos)

1 tbs lemon juice

1 tbs chia "oil" - see recipe below

1 medium red chili, seeded and chopped small

⅓ tsp coconut sugar (or raw sugar/cane juice sugar)

¼ tsp paprika

1 clove garlic, crushed

¼ tsp dried sage, ground

⅛ tsp coarse celtic sea salt

Chia "Oil":

¼ cup white chia seeds

1 ¼ cup water

Corn Salsa:

2 corn cobs, kernels

½ Spanish onion, sliced or diced

1-2 small limes, juiced

1 small avocado, cubed

½ small red bell pepper, sliced or diced

⅓ handful fresh cilantro or other fresh herbs, sliced

salt and pepper to taste

SERVINGS: 4 SKEWERS

INSTRUCTIONS

1 Before starting, make the chia "oil". Combine the chia seeds and water in a screw top jar and shake every few minutes until it forms a gel. Blend in a blender for about a minute and use this instead of oil in recipes. Keep in refrigerator and use as needed within a week.

2 Mix all of the marinade ingredients together in a small bowl or container with a lid.

Add the jackfruit and lightly stir through. Leave to marinade for at least 3 hours or overnight.

3 Once marinated, carefully thread the jackfruit pieces onto metal skewers and place on a baking tray lined with non-stick parchment paper.

Pour half of the marinade liquid over the top.

Bake in oven at 200°C/400°F for 15 minutes, turn over, baste with remaining marinade and bake for another 15 minutes or until browned to your liking.

4 While the skewers are baking, prepare the salsa. Simply mix all of the ingredients together. Yum!

 RECIPE NOTES

This tastes great with some sriracha or other type of hot sauce drizzled over the top.

POTATO & LENTIL DAHL

Affordable, tasty and loaded with iron!

INGREDIENTS

2 cups dried red lentils
(375g/13oz)
4 medium potatoes,
peeled and diced
6 cups water
1 onion, diced
1 large tomato, diced
1 tsp turmeric, ground
1 tsp garam masala
1 tsp ground coriander
Salt and pepper to taste
Rice or vegetables to serve

Topping Suggestions:
Dried or fresh chili, fresh
cilantro, fresh tomato,
lemon juice

SERVINGS: 4

INSTRUCTIONS

1 Put lentils, potatoes and water in a pot over high heat. Stir and bring to a boil. Turn heat down and simmer on low heat for about 10 to 15 minutes until the potatoes are almost soft.

2 Add onion, tomato and spices and mix through. Simmer until onions and potatoes are soft and cooked through (approximately 15 minutes).

3 Serve with cooked rice or vegetables and top with any optional toppings of your choice.

4 Squeeze fresh lemon juice over the top to serve.

CURRIED SINGAPORE NOODLES

A lunchtime favorite!

INGREDIENTS

1 medium red bell pepper (capsicum)
¼ cup scallions, sliced
1 - 2 cloves garlic, chopped
¼ cup frozen peas
1 tsp tomato paste
2 tsp curry powder
⅛ tsp turmeric powder
⅛ tsp white pepper
120g/4oz rice vermicelli noodles, cooked and drained
½ cup vegetable stock
Salt and chili, optional to taste

SERVINGS: 2

INSTRUCTIONS

1 Heat a non-stick fry pan over medium-high heat. Add peppers and stir until softened.

2 Add scallions and stir through again.

3 Add garlic and stir through for a minute or so. Then add the frozen peas and continue to stir through for another minute.

4 Add tomato paste and spices and continue to stir for another minute.

5 Toss through the noodles and add the vegetable stock to loosen everything from the pan and stir through until everything is well combined.

6 Top with chili if you like and serve.

CURRY FRIED RICE

Fried Rice without Oil!
Kids and adults love it... easy, fast and tasty.

INGREDIENTS

3 cloves garlic grated or minced

3 tsp ginger grated

¼ cup vegetable stock

1 whole Spanish onion chopped

½ cup peas (frozen peas are fine)

½ cup corn kernels (frozen corn is fine)

3 tbs scallions sliced

3 cups rice (I used white organic, but brown is best!)

1 tbs curry powder

 RECIPE NOTES

TIP: Add salt, pepper, seasonings, soy sauce, sesame oil, chili flakes etc to give it the extra kick you want!

SERVINGS: 4

INSTRUCTIONS

1 Firstly, get your rice cooking via your favorite method.

2 Next you will need a large fry pan and a wooden spoon.

3 While the pan is cold add the garlic, ginger and Spanish onion. Slowly bring the pan up to a high temperature stirring the ingredients constantly.

4 Once the onions/garlic start to soften, gradually add the peas, corn and scallions and cook through using stock as required to prevent sticking and burning.

5 Finally add the curry powder and cook for approximately 1 minute enjoying that curry aroma before adding the last of your stock.

6 Turn the heat down to low on your cook top and add your freshly cooked and drained rice. Work the mixture through so you get that nice yellow curry color through the rice.

NO COOK ASIAN STIR FRY

So fast to make, so YUMMY to eat!

INGREDIENTS

4 cups mixed vegetables chopped into small pieces (I used broccoli, red peppers, Chinese cabbage and bok choy)

2 cups mushrooms, sliced

1-2 tbs sesame seeds

½ tsp garlic powder

½ tsp onion powder

1 tbs paprika

¼ cup tamari (or soy sauce/ Braggs aminos)

½ tsp coarse celtic sea salt

1 tbs maple syrup

¼ tsp chili flakes (optional, to taste)

Black pepper to taste

SERVINGS: 2 - 4

INSTRUCTIONS

1 Put all chopped vegetables and sliced mushrooms into a large mixing bowl.

2 Add all of the remaining ingredients, stir through thoroughly or mix through with hands.

3 Cover with plastic wrap (or a shower cap like I do) and let sit for at least 3 to 4 hours to bring out the juices and soften the vegetables.

4 Serve with rice, noodles, on toast or just eat as is. Simple and YUM!

 RECIPE NOTES

I let this marinate at room temperature so it is ready to eat with warm noodles or rice.

You can sit it in the refrigerator if you don't mind the mixture being cold.

You can reheat later or eat as a salad too!

ASIAN CHESTNUT NOODLE STIR FRY

A stir fry with a different kind of crunch!

INGREDIENTS

Vegetables:

1 head broccoli, cut into thumb size florets

1 can (227g/8oz) sliced water chestnuts, drained

100g/3.5oz mushrooms, sliced

⅛ cup sliced scallions

Sauce:

¼ cup tamari (or soy sauce/Braggs aminos)

1 tsp grated ginger

½ tsp coarse celtic sea salt

2 tbs thick apricot fruit conserve/jam

1 cup vegetable stock

2 tbs cornstarch

To Serve:

Rice noodles or plain rice cooked.

Sesame seeds, to taste

Chili flakes, to taste

SERVINGS: 2

INSTRUCTIONS

1 Combine all of the sauce ingredients in a screw top jar and shake until well combined. Set aside.

2 Set a wok or non-stick fry pan over high heat and stir fry the vegetables until they have softened and the mushrooms have released their juices. If they stick to the pan, just add a tablespoon or two of water.

3 Add the sauce mixture and stir for another minute or two until the sauce has slightly thickened and has coated the vegetables.

4 Remove from heat and serve over rice noodles or plain rice.

5 Sprinkle with sesame seeds and chili flakes to taste.

BAKED RICE PAPER POCKETS

Hearty Asian pockets with a sriracha kick

INGREDIENTS

½ head broccoli, cut into pieces and steamed
4 boiled potatoes, mashed
1 clove garlic, sliced
1 tsp dried parsley
2 tsp smoked paprika
⅛ tsp black pepper
Salt to taste
1 avocado, sliced
8 large round rice paper sheets

Sriracha Dipping Sauce:

1 tbs sriracha
1 tbs tamari (or soy sauce/ Braggs aminos)
1 tbs lime juice
1 tsp maple syrup

 RECIPE NOTES

Add fresh herbs or anything you like to vary the flavor of your parcels.

SERVINGS: 8 POCKETS

INSTRUCTIONS

1 Mash all of the main ingredients together (except the avocado and rice paper) and set aside.

2 Prepare the Sriracha dipping sauce by mixing all of the ingredients in a small bowl or screw top jar. Set aside.

3 Soften the rice paper sheets one at a time in some warm water. I use a large round baking tray that I can lay the rice paper in. As soon as it feels slightly soft, remove from water and lay on a damp tea towel.

4 Lay a couple of slices of avocado into the center of the rice paper sheet. Put ⅛ of the vegetable mixture over the top and shape into a square shape. Fold the rice paper over to form a small parcel.

5 Place onto a baking tray lined with non-stick parchment paper.

6 Bake in oven at 200°C/400°F for 25 minutes, or until brown and crispy.

7 Serve immediately with sriracha dipping sauce.

DUMPLINGS IN HEARTY ASIAN BROTH

Easy to make and looks impressive!

INGREDIENTS

16 wonton wrappers (palm sized)

1 tofu chili filling (recipe page 87)

Sliced green scallions, for serving decoration

Broth:

6 cups water or vegetable broth

2 tsp coarse celtic sea salt, or to taste

½ tsp white pepper

½ cup nutritional yeast

2 nori sheets, cut into 1 inch/2.5cm squares

chili flakes, to taste

 RECIPE NOTES

Great to eat using asian soup spoons!

SERVINGS: 4

INSTRUCTIONS

1. To prepare the broth, place all of the broth ingredients in a pot and bring to a boil. Turn off the heat and let sit on the hot plate for 5 to 10 minutes with the residual heat.

2. For the dumplings, put 1 to 2 tsp of the tofu chili filling in the center of each wonton wrapper and gently bring corners together and twist in the center to seal.

3. Place wontons in a steamer (on non-stick parchment paper if possible) over hot boiling water for about 15 minutes until cooked.

4. Divide the broth up evenly into 4 shallow soup bowls and sit the dumplings in the center of each bowl.

5. Top with sliced scallions and serve.

THAI RED CURRY

If I could only eat one dish in this book, this would be it!

INGREDIENTS

1 medium onion, sliced lengthways

1 small red bell pepper, sliced

10 green beans, top and tailed and sliced in half

1-2 tsp red Thai curry paste (make sure it is vegan without fish)

2 medium potatoes, par-boiled or par-steamed and cut into wedges

⅓ handful fresh Thai basil leaves (or fresh cilantro/coriander)

1 kaffir lime leaf, very finely sliced

2 inch/5cm lemon grass stalks

1 tbs tamari (or soy sauce/Braggs aminos)

1 cup vegetable stock

2 tsp coconut sugar

¼ cup coconut milk

2 cups rice, cooked

1 small lemon

Topping Suggestions:

Fresh cilantro, fresh sliced chilies, lemon/lime wedges

SERVINGS: 2

INSTRUCTIONS

1 Place the onion into a non-stick frying pan over high heat. Stir until it starts to brown. Add a tablespoon or two of water if necessary to stop the onion from sticking until it turns golden. Add the red bell peppers and green beans and continue to stir for a couple of minutes.

2 Add the curry paste and stir through.

3 Toss in the potatoes, basil leaves, kaffir, lemon grass, tamari and stock. Stir through thoroughly.

4 Add the sugar and coconut milk and continue to cook until the potatoes are soft and the sauce has reduced a little.

5 Remove from heat and serve over rice. Squeeze over some fresh lemon juice when serving.

 RECIPE NOTES

For a lower fat version, use a low fat plant milk such as rice milk and add coconut essence instead of using pure coconut milk.

TOFU SCRAMBLE FRIED RICE

Protein & Carb heaven with no OIL!

INGREDIENTS

Tofu Scramble Mix

½ large onion sliced lengthways

300g/10.5oz firm tofu, crumbled

1 tbs nutritional yeast flakes

¼ tsp black pepper

½ tsp turmeric

½ tsp onion powder

½ tsp garlic powder

Vegetable and Rice Mix

½ medium carrot, peeled and diced into small cubes

½ cup peas (I used frozen)

2 cups cooked rice

Sauce Mix

2 tbs coconut aminos (or 1 tbs tamari and 1 tbs rice vinegar)

½ tsp smoked paprika

1 tsp sesame oil, optional

1 tbs coconut sugar

1 tbs miso paste

2 tbs water

½ tsp chili flakes (or to taste)

1 clove garlic minced or chopped finely

½ tsp coarse celtic sea salt

½ tsp black pepper, ground

 RECIPE NOTES

Use any vegetables that you like. If you don't like tofu you could try mushrooms.

SERVINGS: 2 - 4

INSTRUCTIONS

Sauce Mix

1 Combine all of the sauce ingredients in a small bowl or screw top jar.

2 Set aside for adding later.

Tofu Scramble

1 Put the sliced onion into a hot non-stick pan or wok. Stir until it turns brown and caramelized. If it does stick, add a touch of water to loosen it off.

2 Add the crumbled tofu and stir through. Again, add a touch of water if it sticks to the bottom of the pan.

3 Add all of the scramble spices and mix through thoroughly.

4 Remove from heat and place in a bowl. Set aside while you cook the rest of the ingredients.

Vegetables and Rice

1 Put peas and carrots in hot pan and stir for a couple of minutes until carrots are done. Add a touch of water if needed.

2 Next, add in the sauce mixture and stir well.

3 Turn heat down to medium and add in the rice. Stir until well combined.

4 Pour the tofu scramble mixture in and stir through again.

5 Take off heat and serve! YUM!

SATAY NOODLES

Oh how I looove Satay!!

INGREDIENTS

200g/7oz thick rice noodles, cooked al dente

250g/9oz mixed vegetables, cut into small pieces (eg. onion, carrot, zucchini, broccoli, scallions, green beans, cabbage)

1 Kaffir lime leaf, finely sliced

Sauce:

1 tsp Thai red curry paste (fish free vegan)

¼ cup peanut butter

2 tbs tamari (or soy sauce/ Braggs aminos)

2 tsp coconut sugar

¼ cup coconut milk

SERVINGS: 2

INSTRUCTIONS

1 Place all of the sauce ingredients in a screw top jar and shake until well combined. Set aside.

2 In a hot wok or non-stick fry pan, stir fry the vegetables and Kaffir lime leaves until tender using only a dash of water if needed, should the vegetables begin to stick to the pan.

3 Stir through the noodles and pour over the sauce. Toss through to combine and heat.

4 Remove from heat and serve.

Snacks & Sides

Almond Cheese P73

Chili Tofu Lettuce Cups P87

No Oil Seasoned Fries P77

CASHEW "CHEESE"

Great for slicing, it melts and is great on vegan pizza - YUM!

INGREDIENTS

1¼ cups plant milk (almond/soy/rice/oat etc)
½ cup raw cashew nuts
3 tbs almond meal
1 tbs lemon juice
3 tbs vegetable stock
2 tbs agar agar powder mixed with ¾ cup boiling water
2 tbs miso paste
1 tsp vegetable stock powder
½ tsp white pepper
½ tsp sea salt (celtic or himalayan)

SERVINGS: 4 SERVES

INSTRUCTIONS

1   Firstly, you're going to need a medium sized saucepan, a blender and some cheese molds.

2   In a separate bowl mix the agar agar with boiling water until you have a smooth paste. Then let it sit for approximately 5 minutes before use.

3   Add all the remaining ingredients and agar agar paste into the blender and blend until smooth.

4   Pour the mixture into a medium size saucepan and gradually bring to the boil before reducing heat to a simmer.

5   After 5-10 minutes the mixture will become very thick and creamy. Quickly pour the mixture into your cheese molds.

6   Place the cheese molds into the refrigerator for 30 minutes or until set.

ALMOND "CHEESE"

Quick, easy and tasty - you won't ever get store bought again!

INGREDIENTS

1¼ cups plant milk eg. almond, oat, rice, soy etc
½ cup blanched almonds (ie. skinless)
1 tbs lemon juice
¼ tsp white pepper
2 tsps coarse celtic sea salt
2 large cloves garlic
1 tbs mixed herbs
1 tbs agar agar powder
2 tbs tapioca starch
½ cup hot boiled water

Coating

1 tbs paprika
1 tbs mixed Italian herbs

SERVINGS: 4 - 6

INSTRUCTIONS

1 Firstly, you are going to need a medium sized saucepan, a blender and some cheese molds (I used mini spring form cake tins but you can use any plastic containers or silicone molds that you have on hand).

2 Add all the ingredients (except the coating mix) into the blender and blend until smooth.

3 Pour the mixture into a medium size saucepan and gradually bring to the boil before reducing heat to a simmer.

4 After 5-10 minutes the mixture will become thick and creamy. Quickly pour the mixture into your cheese molds.

5 Place the cheese molds into the refrigerator for 30 minutes or until set.

6 Remove from molds and carefully roll in the coating mix to coat the edges - this makes the cheese look great and taste even better!

NUT FREE SMOKED PAPRIKA "CHEESE"

It slices and grates...
and is a nut free plant based cheese!
WOW!

INGREDIENTS

Cheese Ingredients

1 cup water
1 cup oats
1 cup sweet potato (kumara) steamed until soft
1 whole roasted red pepper (capsicum) marinated in vinegar
½ cup nutritional yeast
⅓ to 1 tbs smoked paprika
2½ tsp coarse celtic sea salt
¼ tsp white pepper
1 tsp onion powder
1 tsp garlic powder
2 tbs lemon juice
1 cup water extra for over top of mixture in blender... you can also add any other spices, herbs etc that you like.

Agar Agar thickener

1⅓ cups water
2½ tbs agar agar powder (or 8tbs agar flakes)

SERVINGS: 8 - 10

INSTRUCTIONS

1 Firstly, you will need a powerful blender or food processor to handle the main ingredients.

2 Add the cheese ingredients to your blender/processor in the order stated.

3 Blend the ingredients until you have a nice smooth cheesy mixture. Have a quick taste test and add extra spice or salt as required.

4 Put the cheese mixture aside for a few minutes while you prepare the Agar Agar.

5 In a medium size saucepan add both the water and Agar Agar powder.

6 Bring the mixture to the boil whilst constantly stirring, then turn down the heat to low and keep stirring until the mixture has a thick molasses type consistency.

7 Once the Agar Agar mixture is ready, transfer it to the cheese mixture in your blender/processor and blend for about 30 seconds until mixture is well combined.

8 Pour the mixture into your favorite cheese mold(s). NB: You can use plastic containers, shallow bowls, cups, quick release cake tins etc.

9 Settle the mixture in your mold(s) so that the surface is flat. This will help the cheese sit flat when you turn it out. If necessary, use a spatula to spread evenly.

10 Pop your mold(s) into the refrigerator for approximately 30 minutes to set and then carefully turn out the cheese onto your favorite serving platter!

HALLOUMI "CHEESE"

This vegan Halloumi cheese recipe is a must for cheese lovers!

INGREDIENTS

- 250g/9oz organic tofu (firm is best)
- 1 tsp onion powder
- 1 tsp paprika powder
- ½ tsp turmeric
- 1 tsp coarse celtic sea salt
- ¼ cup nutritional yeast
- ¼ cup boiling water (from boiled kettle)

 RECIPE NOTES

You can also bake these in an oven or an air fryer until cooked to your liking.

SERVINGS: 4

INSTRUCTIONS

1 Place tofu into freezer overnight.

2 Remove tofu from freezer and let thaw in refrigerator.

3 Press liquid from tofu by placing it between two chopping boards and putting something heavy on top to weigh it down.

Note: Make sure you put a tea towel underneath to catch the run-off.

4 Pat the tofu dry and slice into ¼ inch (½ cm) slices.

5 Prepare your marinade by combining remaining ingredients in a bowl until well combined and smooth.

6 Baste tofu slices on both sides and if you have time, let marinade for at least a couple of hours or overnight.

7 Heat non-stick pan on high/medium-high and cook on each side until golden and crispy (about 2 minutes on each side).

8 Cook until all halloumi slices are done... serve and enjoy! AWESOME - Halloumi alternative without the Dairy!

NUT FREE "CHEESE" SAUCE

A no oil vegan RICH, CREAMY cheese sauce recipe

INGREDIENTS

- 1½ cups water
- ½ cup oats
- 270g/9.5oz (½ medium head) cauliflower, steamed till soft
- 1 whole roasted red pepper (store bought marinated)
- ¼ cup nutritional yeast
- 1 tsp smoked paprika
- 2 tsp coarse celtic sea salt
- ½ tsp white pepper
- 2 tsp garlic powder
- 1 tbs miso paste (white)
- 2 tbs tahini
- 2 tbs lemon juice
- ½ cup unsweetened plant milk (almond/soy/rice/oat etc)

SERVINGS: 4 - 8 SERVES

INSTRUCTIONS

1 The main thing you will need for this recipe is a blender.

2 Add all the ingredients to the blender and blend for 1-2 minutes and it's ready to serve.

 RECIPE NOTES

This sauce is really versatile.

It's ideal for nachos, lasagne, pasta sauces and pretty much anywhere you need a cheese sauce!

NO OIL SEASONED FRIES

Super awesome fries without oil!

INGREDIENTS

5 large potatoes
½ tsp onion powder
½ tsp garlic powder
1 tsp mixed Italian herbs
2 tbs polenta/coarse corn meal
1 tbs corn starch (or arrowroot)
½ tsp coarse celtic sea salt (or salt of your choice)
¼ tsp white pepper
2 tsp tamari (or soy sauce/ Braggs aminos)

 RECIPE NOTES

Serve and enjoy with vegan mayonnaise, ketchup, mustard, pesto, sweet chili sauce, gravy etc.

SERVINGS: 2

INSTRUCTIONS

1 Preheat oven to 180°C/360°F.

2 Peel and wash your potatoes and cut into even small finger sized shapes.

3 Place in a large mixing bowl.

4 Add all remaining ingredients and mix together well - preferably by hand so that the fries get coated evenly.

5 Place on a baking tray lined with non-stick parchment paper.

6 Place in oven for 10 to 15 minutes then remove and turn the fries over.

7 Place back in oven for another 15 minutes or until desired crispness is reached.

HERBED MASH POTATOES

Creamy, filling and dairy free.

INGREDIENTS

4-6 potatoes (peeled & chopped into bite size pieces)

¼ tsp turmeric (for color more than taste)

¼ tsp white pepper, or to taste

⅜ tsp sage ground dried

1 tsp marjoram dried

1 tsp basil dried

1 tsp coarse celtic sea salt to taste

Note:

Consider the herbs & spices above a guide only. Add whatever you like, especially if you have your own fresh herbs growing!

INSTRUCTIONS

1 Firstly, you will need a large pot and a potato masher or immersion blender.

2 Wash, peel and chop the potatoes before placing in a suitable large pot. Fill pot with water so that it just covers the potatoes.

3 Add all the other ingredients to the pot, mix, then place on your stove a high heat with the lid off.

4 Once boiling, reduce the heat to a high simmer for approximately 10 minutes or until potatoes are soft.

5 When the potatoes are ready drain the excess liquid (broth) off into a large bowl. Keep this broth for use in the mashing/whipping process and any excess can be used as a vegetable broth base for other recipes.

6 At this point you're ready to mash or whip. Depending on your taste preferences you might want to remove any larger fresh herbs or spices you added earlier. When ready, use immersion blender to work through the potatoes adding a ladle of cooking broth back as required to keep the mash moist.

7 When the mash consistency suits your taste it's ready to serve!

OVEN ROASTED BAKED POTATOES

It's hard to imagine anything better.

INGREDIENTS

8 medium to large boiled potatoes
1 handful garlic cloves in their skin
⅛ cup vegetable stock
2 tsp corn starch
2 tsp dried sage leaves or herbs of choice
Coarse celtic sea salt to taste
Black Pepper to taste

 RECIPE NOTES

I boil my potatoes in their skins for about 45 minutes. I then drain them and immediately peel the skins off under cold water. This is such an easy way to remove the skin.

SERVINGS: 2 - 4

INSTRUCTIONS

1 Preheat your oven to 190°C/380°F.

2 Once you have boiled and peeled your potatoes using your preferred cooking method, cut them in halves or quarters and place them on a baking tray that has been lined with some non-stick parchment paper.

3 Use a cake server or base of a pot to squish the potatoes down a bit. By flattening them out, you will increase the surface area of the potatoes and add more edges for extra crispiness.

4 Now mix together the vegetable stock, corn starch and dried herbs. Then pour evenly over all of the potatoes.

5 Scatter the garlic cloves evenly across the tray also. These can be pushed out of the skins once cooked and taste sweet, juicy and delicious.

6 Season with salt and pepper.

7 Place in oven for approximately 45 minutes or until your desired level of crispiness has been reached. Enjoy!

LEMON POTATOES

Citrus Potato Bliss!

INGREDIENTS

1 onion, diced
6 medium potatoes, cubed
1 cup vegetable stock
1 small handful fresh lemon thyme (or basil)
2 pinches coarse celtic sea salt
½ fresh lemon

 RECIPE NOTES

You could crisp these up in the oven at 180°C / 360°F for about 10 to 15 minutes.

SERVINGS: 2 - 4

INSTRUCTIONS

1 Place the onion into a non-stick frying pan over high heat. Stir until it starts to brown. Add a tablespoon or two of water to stop the onion from sticking until it turns golden. Add the potatoes and stir through until well combined.

2 Add the vegetable stock to the pan and stir through. Add thyme and salt. Leave on high heat and stir every few minutes until the potatoes are tender (approximately 12 minutes).

3 Remove from heat and let sit for a few minutes with a lid on.

4 When ready to serve squeeze the juice of half a fresh lemon over the top.

CREAMY LEMON DIJON POTATO SALAD

Potato Salad is yummy.
Potato salad with this sauce is divine!

INGREDIENTS

1 kg/2 pounds potatoes, cooked & sliced or diced

2 tbs capers, chopped

4 tbs pickles/gherkins, chopped

1 small Spanish onion, thinly sliced

1 tbs fresh parsley, chopped

Dressing:

1 cup water

1 cup plant milk (rice/almond/soy)

2 tsp coarse celtic sea salt

¼ tsp ground sage

¼ tsp white pepper

1 tbs nutritional yeast, optional

2 tbs cornstarch

4 tbs lemon juice

1 tsp dijon mustard

¼ cup pinenuts

SERVINGS: 4 - 6

INSTRUCTIONS

1 Before you begin, prepare your dressing. Place all of the dressing ingredients in a pot (except the pinenuts) and bring to a boil. Reduce heat and simmer for 5 minutes or until slightly thickened.

2 Let cool and place in a blender with the pinenuts. Blend until nice and creamy.

3 Place all of the non-dressing ingredients in a large bowl. Pour your dressing over the potato mixture and combine gently.

4 You can either eat as is, or take about ¼ of this mixture and put it in your blender to make an extra thick dressing. Once blended, pour this back over the salad for a thick and rich potato salad.

 RECIPE NOTES

Boil potatoes in their skin until cooked through. Then hold under cold water and the peels will just pull away using your fingers.

CREAMY CAULIFLOWER

Simple, fast and tasty.

SERVINGS: 2 - 4

INGREDIENTS

1 medium cauliflower including core, cut into bite size pieces

Sauce:
¼ cup pinenuts
1 tsp coarse celtic sea salt
1 tbs white vinegar or lemon juice
⅛ tsp white pepper
½ cup boiled hot water
1 clove garlic

 RECIPE NOTES

Great sprinkled with Almond Parmesan page 95.

INSTRUCTIONS

1 Steam the cauliflower florets and core pieces till soft to your liking.

2 Once steamed, add the stem pieces and some of the cauliflower (about 1 cup worth) into a blender or food processor along with all of the sauce ingredients. Blend until creamy.

3 Place the remaining cauliflower into an oven proof dish and pour the sauce over the top.

4 Sprinkle with paprika or nutmeg and serve as is, or bake at 180°C/360°F for 10 to 15 minutes.

MIDDLE EASTERN CAULIFLOWER

Is there a better way to serve cauliflower?

INGREDIENTS

1 medium head cauliflower, chopped into small bite size pieces

3 dates, pitted and chopped

2 tbs pinenuts

1 tsp cumin

¼ cup vegetable stock

2 tsp lemon juice

Salt and pepper to taste

Sumac, for sprinkling over dish.

SERVINGS: 2

INSTRUCTIONS

1 Place the cauliflower into a non-stick frying pan over high heat. Stir until it starts to soften. Add a tablespoon or two of water to stop the cauliflower from sticking until it turns lightly golden.

2 Add dates, pinenuts and cumin to the pan and stir for another minute.

3 Pour vegetable stock into the pan and stir through until mixture is well combined and the cauliflower has softened to your liking.

4 Remove from heat and season with salt and pepper.

5 Squeeze over some fresh lemon juice and sprinkle with sumac to serve.

VEGETABLE PARCELS

Makes individual serves - create as many as you like!

INGREDIENTS

Main Ingredient Suggestions:

Cabbage, sliced
Scallions, sliced
Carrot, sliced
Garlic, chopped
Mushrooms, sliced
Black beans, cooked and drained
Rice, pre-cooked
Noodles, pre-cooked
Sesame Seeds

Add In Suggestions:

Tamari (or soy sauce/ Braggs aminos)
Pasta Sauce
Ketchup
Pesto
Chili Flakes
Hot Sauce
Maple Syrup
Coconut Sugar
Lemon Juice
Herbs
Spices

 RECIPE NOTES

Asian combination - cabbage, scallions, carrot, garlic, mushrooms, black beans, rice, sesame seeds, mixed with soy sauce, maple syrup and chili flakes.

Italian combination - potatoes, garlic, scallions, mushrooms, mixed with Italian sauce, dried herbs, fennel seeds and pepper.

SERVINGS: VARIES

INSTRUCTIONS

1 This is more of a guide than a recipe. You can use any combination of vegetables and flavorings that you like and make little baked parcels that taste delicious.

2 Start by cutting non-stick parchment paper into 12 inch/30cm squares. You will also need some heat proof baking string or some aluminum foil folded into long strips that can be used to tie the parcels up.

3 Place any combination of vegetables and add ins into each parcel. Bring the sides together, twist and tie up with string or aluminum foil. Put the parcels on a baking tray and bake at 180°C/360°F for about 45 minutes.

4 Carefully open your parcel and be careful for steam coming out. Serve and enjoy.

5 To watch a video demonstration of this, please visit: https://cookingwithplants. com/recipe/easy-baked-vegetable-parcels/

84

MINI QUICHES

Great for picnics or a tasty snack.

INGREDIENTS

- ⅓ cup chickpea flour
- ½ tsp baking soda
- ¼ cup cashews
- ½ cup oats
- 1 cup soy milk (or plant milk of choice)
- 3 tbs white vinegar
- 2 cloves garlic
- 1 tsp coarse celtic sea salt
- 1 tsp himalayan black salt
- 1 tsp mustard

Optional Topping Suggestions:

Sliced mushrooms, chopped red peppers, sliced onion, herbs, chili flakes

SERVINGS: 10 - 12 QUICHES

INSTRUCTIONS

1 Preheat oven to 180°C/360°F.

2 Line a muffin tin with squares of non-stick parchment paper that have been run under water to make it easy to shape into each hole of the tray.

3 Add all ingredients (except toppings) to a blender and blend until smooth.

4 Pour the batter into each muffin hole and top with preferred toppings as outlined in the optional toppings list.

5 Bake for 20 - 30 mins.

6 Let sit at room temperature for 10 to 15 minutes, or cool completely.

7 Can be eaten hot or cold.

ASPARAGUS PUFFS

Puff Pastry + Asparagus = Delicious.

INGREDIENTS

12 spears asparagus washed and dry end snapped off

3 sheets puff pastry (dairy and egg free vegan pastry)

1 tsp paprika powder

SERVINGS: 12 PUFFS

INSTRUCTIONS

1 Pre-heat oven to 175°C/350°F.

2 Wash, dry and snap ends of asparagus.

3 Cut pastry sheets into quarters and leave on plastic so it doesn't stick to the bench while you're working with it.

4 Wrap each asparagus spear from one corner to the other on a 45 degree angle.

5 Place rolled asparagus spears on a baking tray lined with non-stick parchment paper.

6 Sprinkle with paprika powder.

7 Bake for about 20 to 25 minutes until crispy and light brown on top. Serve immediately.

CHILI TOFU LETTUCE CUPS

Even tastier than they look!

INGREDIENTS

½ small onion, sliced lengthways

450g/16oz firm organic tofu, crumbled

1 tbs tamari (or soy sauce/ Braggs aminos)

¼ cup vegetable stock

1 tsp chili flakes, or to taste

1 tsp coconut sugar

⅛ red bell pepper, sliced

1 tsp fresh ginger, grated

½ bunch fresh Thai basil leaves, chopped

Salt and pepper to taste

½ fresh lemon

Fresh romaine/cos lettuce leaves

SERVINGS: 2 - 4

INSTRUCTIONS

1 Place the onion into a non-stick frying pan over high heat. Stir until it starts to brown. Add a tablespoon or two of water to stop the onion from sticking until it turns golden.

2 Add tofu and stir through.

3 Add red bell pepper and stir through.

4 Add vegetable stock and tamari and stir through for a minute or two until well combined and pan is deglazed.

5 Add remaining ingredients (except lemon and lettuce) and stir over high heat for 5 to 10 minutes until the mixture is quite dry and the bell pepper is soft and cooked through.

6 Remove from heat and squeeze fresh lemon juice over the top.

7 Put in lettuce cups and serve.

NO OIL HUMMUS

A rich creamy cholesterol free recipe.
Great for parties, snacks....anytime!

INGREDIENTS

1 425g/15oz can chickpeas, drained and brine reserved

1 425g/15oz can cannellini beans , drained and brine reserved

2 cloves garlic

1 whole lemon juiced

1 tsp cumin powder

1 tsp coarse celtic sea salt

¼ tsp white pepper

2 tbs tahini

¼ to ⅓ cup drained chickpea/cannellini bean brine

SERVINGS: 4 - 6

INSTRUCTIONS

1 All you need for this recipe is a good food processor/blender and a bowl or container to store your Hummus.

2 Put all the ingredients in the food processor and blend for about 30 seconds.

Note: If making in a blender you may need more of the drained can juices to get the right consistency for the hummus.

3 Pour the hummus into a serving bowl and sprinkle with some whole chick peas, cumin seeds and paprika. Serve with crackers, bell peppers, carrot & celery sticks, then sit back and munch away!

GREEK SPICED EGGPLANT HUMMUS

A delicious alternative to classic Hummus

INGREDIENTS

2 large eggplants, halved lengthways

1 400g/14oz can chickpeas, with juices (not drained)

2 tsp dried basil

2 tsp dried oregano

1 tsp dried parsley

½ tsp dried rosemary

2 tbs tahini

2 tbs lemon juice

2 cloves garlic

1 tsp coarse celtic sea salt, or to taste

¼ tsp black pepper, or to taste

SERVINGS: 6 - 8

INSTRUCTIONS

1 Place eggplant halves face down onto a baking tray lined with non-stick parchment paper.

2 Bake skin side up at 175°C/350°F for 45 minutes or until the eggplant is soft.

3 Remove eggplants from oven and let cool for 10 minutes. Scoop out the flesh and dispose of the eggplant skin.

4 Combine cooked eggplant and all other ingredients in a food processor and pulse until smooth and creamy.

RUSTIC BREAD STICKS

Perfect with soup, yummy with hummus!

INGREDIENTS

Yeast Ingredients

3 tsp Instant Yeast

1 tsp Brown Rice Syrup (or agave/maple syrup)

⅛ cup Warm Water

Bread Ingredients

2 cups flour unbleached bread flour or all purpose flour

1 cup whole wheat flour or all purpose

¾ cup warm water

1 tbs tahini

⅛ tsp coarse celtic sea salt

⅛ tsp garlic powder

2 tsp mixed Italian herbs

2 tbs nutritional yeast

SERVINGS: 13 STICKS

INSTRUCTIONS

1. Mix yeast ingredients in a bowl and leave for 5 minutes until yeast activates and becomes bubbly.

2. Once yeast mixture is ready, add all bread ingredients and stir the mixture together until it forms a loose dough. It won't take more than a few minutes!

3. Once all the dough starts to lift away from the bowl use your hands to form the dough into a ball.

4. Cover the bowl/dough with a tea towel and let it sit in a warm draught free area for 1-4 hours until dough has doubled in size.

5. Once dough is ready, preheat the oven to 200C/400F.

6. Get a baking tray and line it with non stick baking paper.

7. Using a bowl of water to wet your hands, break off small chunks of dough and work them into bread stick shapes and place them on the baking tray about a finger width apart until the tray is full.

8. If you wish, now is a great time to coat the bread sticks with your choice of seeds, salt, olives etc. You could also coat the sticks with some plant milk if you are looking for a shiny brown finish.

9. When your tray is ready, pop it in the oven for 6 minutes.

10. After 6 minutes pull the sticks out and turn them over before returning to the oven for a further 6 minutes or until browned to your liking.

11. Serve with your favorite sides, dips, soups!

MAPLE SPICED OVEN ROASTED NUTS

One of the best tasting snacks ever!

INGREDIENTS

2 cups mixed seeds and nuts (not pinenuts) I used:

¼ cup sesame seeds
¼ cup pumpkin seeds
½ cup cashews
½ cup blanched almonds
½ cup sunflower seeds
2 tbs maple syrup
½ tsp cinnamon
½ tsp ginger
½ tsp coarse celtic sea salt
¼ tsp garam masala

RECIPE NOTES

Store in a glass jar with a screw top lid at room temperature or in the refrigerator. Great on cereal (or even as a granola)!

SERVINGS: 2 CUPS

INSTRUCTIONS

1 Preheat oven to 175°C/350°F and line a baking tray with non-stick parchment paper.

2 Place all the ingredients in a mixing bowl and stir until well combined.

3 Pour on parchment paper and spread evenly. Bake in middle of oven for 15 minutes.

4 Let cool for about half an hour (if you can wait that long) and break apart into bite size pieces. Enjoy!

Condiments

Sauces, dressings & dips

Mushroom Gravy P105

Hoisin Sauce P111

Tzatziki P97

SALT FREE GARLIC & HERB SEASONING

Maximum flavor with NO salt!

INGREDIENTS

¼ tsp chili flakes
1 tbs garlic powder
2 tsp onion powder
1 tsp dried parsley
1 tsp fennel seeds
1 tsp cumin seeds
1 tsp mustard seeds
1 tsp dried rosemary
1 tsp celery seeds
1 tsp dried thyme
1 tsp dried coriander
1 tsp ground black pepper

SERVINGS: VARIES

INSTRUCTIONS

1. Place all of the ingredients in a coffee grinder, small blender or small food processor and grind down.

2. Keep in a screw top jar or a herb container and use to season your favorite dishes without salt.

ALMOND PARMESAN "CHEESE"

Delicious on pasta, risotto and vegetables!

INGREDIENTS

1 tbs nutritional yeast
¼ cup almonds
1 tsp coarse celtic sea salt

SERVINGS: 4 - 8

INSTRUCTIONS

1 Add all of the almond parmesan ingredients into a small blender, coffee grinder or small food processor and pulse until ground up.

2 Keep in a screw top jar or a herb container and use in place of traditional parmesan cheese.

CHARGRILLED RED PEPPER PESTO

Perfect for salads, pasta or even as a dip!

INGREDIENTS

1 whole chargrilled red pepper (store bought, marinated in a vinegar and salt brine)

2 handfuls baby spinach

1 bunch basil (approx. 60g/2oz worth)

¼ cup almonds (or nuts of choice - eg pinenuts, cashews etc)

2 tbs nutritional yeast flakes

½ tsp coarse celtic sea salt

1 clove garlic

2 tbs lemon juice

INSTRUCTIONS

1 Get your food processor ready (you can use a blender but you will need more liquid such as vegetable stock to get it mixing properly).

2 Add all of the ingredients into your food processor and pulse a few times. Then let run for about 5 to 10 seconds until well chopped and combined.

3 Stop the machine and scrape down the sides of the food processor bowl so that all the ingredients are well mixed and chopped thoroughly.

4 Repeat this process if you want the mixture finer. It is up to you how chunky you would like it.

5 Serve and enjoy!!

TZATZIKI

Delicious with ANYTHING!!!

INGREDIENTS

3 tbs scallions, chopped - optional

¼ cup water

1 cup cashews

1 tbs lemon juice

1 tsp coarse celtic sea salt

Add Ins:

1 small Lebanese cucumber (60g/2oz), cubed small

2 cloves garlic, crushed

SERVINGS: 1 CUP

INSTRUCTIONS

1 Place all of the main ingredients in a blender and blend until smooth.

2 Pour mixture into a bowl and add the cucumber and garlic. Stir well. Best chilled to let the flavors combine and intensify.

 RECIPE NOTES

Great served with boiled or baked potatoes.

SMOKY RED BELL PEPPER DIP

Looks great and tastes amazing!

INGREDIENTS

6 medium red bell peppers, thinly sliced
5 large cloves garlic
1 tbs white vinegar
1 tsp coarse celtic sea salt
¼ cup water
1 tsp cornstarch
1 tsp hot sauce, optional
Pepper to taste

SERVINGS: 2 CUPS

INSTRUCTIONS

1 Dry fry the bell peppers in a hot non-stick pan, using a bit of water if needed to prevent sticking.

2 You will hear popping and very slight char-grilling will occur.

3 Keep stirring until the bell peppers are softened.

4 Remove from heat and put into a blender or food processor with remaining ingredients. Blend to your desired consistency (you can leave it chunky or make it smooth).

5 Put the mixture in a pot and bring to a boil, reduce to a low simmer. Cook for 30 minutes without a lid and stir occasionally.

6 Remove from heat and serve warm or put into screw top jars and keep in the refrigerator to serve cold.

This will keep in the refrigerator for a week or two.

GUACAMOLE

Simple, but so full of flavor.
I think I could live on it!

INGREDIENTS

2 avocados
2 tbs lime juice
1 small Spanish onion, chopped
2 cloves garlic, crushed
Salt and pepper to taste
Chili flakes or fresh sliced chili (optional)

SERVINGS: 2 - 4

INSTRUCTIONS

1 Mash avocados in a bowl and add the remaining ingredients. Mix well and serve.

OIL FREE VEGAN MAYONNAISE

This tasty tofu mayonnaise is lovely and creamy and great on sandwiches and burgers!

INGREDIENTS

280g/10oz organic tofu (I like organic firm tofu best, but you can use silken tofu if preferred)

1 tbs lemon juice

1 tsp apple cider vinegar

1 tsp dijon mustard

1 tbs raw sugar

1 tsp coarse celtic sea salt

⅛ tsp white pepper

2 tbs soy milk

SERVINGS: 8 - 12

INSTRUCTIONS

1 For this recipe all you need is an appropriately sized blender or food processor.

2 Place all the ingredients in the blender except for the soy milk. Blend for approximately 1 minute until the mixture is smooth.

3 If the mixture seems too thick add half the soy milk and blend again. Keep adding milk until you are happy with the texture.

Note: If using silken tofu you probably won't need the extra soy milk :-)

CASHEW SOUR CREAM

So fast and simple to make... and
SUPER TASTY!

INGREDIENTS

1 cup cashews
¼ to ⅓ cup water
1 tsp coarse celtic sea salt
1 tbs lemon juice

SERVINGS: VARIES

INSTRUCTIONS

1   Place all ingredients in a blender and blend until thick and creamy.

2   Best served chilled.

WHITE SAUCE

Great with Potatoes, Cauliflower and most veggies.

INGREDIENTS

3 cups plant milk
(almond/soy/rice/oat)
4 tbs cornstarch
1 tsp coarse celtic sea salt
Dash of nutmeg

Optional Extras:
1 tbs dried herbs

SERVINGS: 4 - 6

INSTRUCTIONS

1 Place all of the ingredients into a pot and mix well before turning on the heat. Once combined, bring to a boil, then lower heat to simmer and continue to stir until thickened.

2 Remove from heat and serve.

 RECIPE NOTES

Mix the cornstarch and some of the plant milk in a screw top jar and shake well to combine. This will prevent lumps from forming in your sauce.

RICH BROWN GRAVY

So good on baked potatoes!

INGREDIENTS

¼ cup tamari (or soy sauce/Braggs aminos)
1 ½ cups vegetable stock
¼ tsp ground sage
1 tbs nutritional yeast
⅛ to ¼ tsp white pepper
3 tbs brown rice flour
Salt to taste

 RECIPE NOTES

Mix the flour and some of the stock in a screw top jar and shake well to combine. This will prevent lumps from forming in your sauce.

SERVINGS: 4 - 6

INSTRUCTIONS

1 Place all of the ingredients into a pot and mix well before turning on the heat.

2 Once combined, bring to a boil, then lower heat to simmer and continue to stir until thickened.

3 Remove from heat and serve.

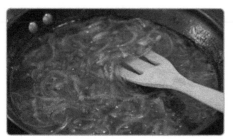

ONION GRAVY

So good we sometimes eat this like soup!

INGREDIENTS

4 medium onions, sliced lengthways
3 cups vegetable stock
1 tsp coarse celtic sea salt
20 grinds of black pepper, or to taste
2 tbs cornstarch
1 tsp lemon juice (optional)

 RECIPE NOTES

This also tastes great as a soup with some fresh crusty bread! Serves 2 when eating it this way!

SERVINGS: 4

INSTRUCTIONS

1 Place the onion into a non-stick frying pan over high heat. Stir until it starts to brown. Add 2 - 3 tablespoons of the stock to loosen the onions.

2 Add cornstarch and stir through until mixture thickens in the pan.

3 Add the rest of the vegetable stock and stir again.

4 Add salt and pepper.

5 Boil for about 5 to 10 minutes and stir till thickened to desired consistency.

6 Remove from heat and stir through the lemon juice (if using).

MUSHROOM GRAVY

Yummy on rice, veggies, toast and pasta

INGREDIENTS

280g/10oz mushrooms, sliced (5 large portobellos)

1 tbs tamari (or soy sauce/Braggs aminos)

2 cups vegetable stock

¼ tsp onion powder

⅛ tsp black pepper

2 - 3 tbs brown rice flour

Salt to taste

 RECIPE NOTES

Mix the flour and some of the stock in a screw top jar and shake well to combine. This will prevent lumps from forming in your sauce.

Portobellos are great to use in a mushroom sauce as they hold their shape more and don't break down to nothing.

SERVINGS: 4 - 6

INSTRUCTIONS

1 Place the mushrooms into a pot over high heat. Stir until the mushrooms release their juices and start to soften. You may need to add a little bit of the stock to stop the mushrooms from sticking to the pot.

2 Place all of the remaining ingredients into the pot and stir through. Once combined, lower heat to simmer and continue to stir until thickened.

3 Remove from heat and serve.

INSTANT CHEESY HERB & GARLIC SAUCE

A fast blend and serve cheese sauce that can also be used as a dip!

INGREDIENTS

1 cup loosely packed fresh basil (or herbs of choice)

2 large garlic cloves

½ cup cashews (or blanched almonds)

½ cup oats

1 tbs white miso paste

½ cup nutritional yeast

1 tsp coarse celtic sea salt

1 tsp Dijon mustard

¼ tsp white pepper, or to taste

1 ½ cups boiled hot water

SERVINGS: 4 - 6

INSTRUCTIONS

1 Place ingredients in blender and blend till smooth, then serve!

 RECIPE NOTES

Toss through pasta immediately or let it cool and use as a dip. Add extra water or plant milk for a thinner sauce.

CREAMY GARLIC SAUCE

Not to be eaten before a hot date!

INGREDIENTS

4 cloves garlic
¼ cup pinenuts
½ tsp coarse celtic sea salt, or to taste
1 tsp lemon juice
¼ cup plant milk (almond/soy/rice/oat)

INSTRUCTIONS

1 Place ingredients in a blender and blend until smooth and creamy.

 RECIPE NOTES

Put on salad and potatoes or serve with falafels. To make this thinner and use as a dressing add a little more plant milk.

5 MINUTE CURRY SAUCE

This sauce is so fast to make, yet super tasty. Ideal for those busy week nights!

INGREDIENTS

½ cup orange juice
⅛ tsp cayenne pepper
1 tsp coarse celtic sea salt
½ tsp white pepper
2 tbs curry powder
1 tbs coconut sugar
⅛ tsp all spice or star anise
3 tbs corn flour
½ cup tomato paste
1 cup vegetable stock
⅔ cup apple juice

SERVINGS: 4

INSTRUCTIONS

1 Before you begin you will need a blender, medium sized saucepan and mixing spoon.

2 First up, add all sauce ingredients into your blender and combine till smooth.

3 Next, pour the mixture into your saucepan and bring to a medium simmer whilst constantly stirring.

4 Now reduce the heat to a low simmer and allow the sauce to thicken to your desired consistency.

5 And that's it! The sauce can now be served with roasted or fried potatoes, over steamed vegetables, as a dipping sauce or even as a base for a curry.

SPICY TOMATO KETCHUP

Tomato Ketchup with a smoky kick!

INGREDIENTS

1 large onion, diced

2 cloves garlic, minced

400g/14oz canned tomatoes, crushed or diced

1 tsp chili flakes, or to taste

2 tbs coconut sugar

¼ cup orange juice

3 tbs white vinegar

¼ cup tamari (or soy sauce/Braggs aminos)

1 tsp celery seeds (or 1 tbs chopped celery)

1 tsp dried thyme

5 dates, pitted and chopped

2 tsp smoked paprika

1 tsp coarse celtic sea salt, or to taste

Pepper to taste

SERVINGS: 1 CUP

INSTRUCTIONS

1 Place the onion and garlic into a non-stick frying pan over high heat. Stir until onion starts to brown.

2 Add tomatoes and chili flakes and stir to combine.

3 Add remaining ingredients and lower heat to medium temperature and stir for another 5 minutes. Turn heat to low and simmer without lid until you reach a consistency that you like (I cooked mine for 30 minutes). Stir occasionally.

4 Remove from heat and let cool.

5 Using a blender or food processor, blend your mixture until smooth.

PEANUT DIPPING SAUCE

Tastes great with just about everything; rice, vegetables, noodles, rice paper parcels etc

INGREDIENTS

2 tbs peanut butter
⅛ cup coconut milk
¼ tsp coarse celtic sea salt
1 tsp coconut sugar
1 tsp tamari (or soy sauce/ Braggs aminos)
¼ tsp hot sauce such as sriracha (optional)
Chili flakes, to taste

SERVINGS: 4 - 6

INSTRUCTIONS

1 Combine all of the ingredients in a bowl or jar with screw top lid and mix together until smooth.

HOISIN SAUCE

A unique flavor that is awesome with Sushi, noodles and rice dishes

INGREDIENTS

¼ cup to ⅓ cup tamari (or soy sauce/Braggs aminos)

1 tbs almond butter

tbs maple syrup (or coconut sugar)

2 tsp coconut aminos (or rice vinegar/white vinegar)

⅛ tsp garlic powder

⅛ tsp ground ginger

1 tsp sesame oil, optional

⅛ tsp hot chili sauce or flakes, or to taste

⅛ tsp ground black pepper

SERVINGS: 4 - 6

INSTRUCTIONS

1 Combine all of the ingredients in a bowl or jar with screw top lid and mix together.

SWEET CHILI CHUTNEY

Spicy, sweet and delicious.
Perfect for any dish needing some Wow factor!

INGREDIENTS

1 whole red bell pepper/capsicum, cored

1 ripe mango, peeled and seed removed

10 large dates (pitted)

1-3 whole red chilies (depending on how hot you like it)

4-6 cloves garlic peeled (or less depending on how garlicky you like it)

1 tsp ginger (freshly grated)

1 tbs apple cider vinegar

1 tsp sea salt (celtic or himalayan)

SERVINGS: 1 CUP

INSTRUCTIONS

1 Put all ingredients into a food processor and pulse to keep it slightly chunky.

2 Pulse till you have a consistency you like.

 RECIPE NOTES

If you do not have access to mango you can use 5 dried apricots instead!

SWEET CHILI DRESSING

Sweet, spicy and delicious on anything needing a flavor kick!

INGREDIENTS

1 whole red pepper (capsicum)
¼ cup maple syrup
1-3 whole red chilies small
4-6 cloves garlic to taste
1 tsp ginger grated
1 tbs apple cider vinegar
1 tsp coarse celtic sea salt

SERVINGS: 6

INSTRUCTIONS

1 For this recipe all you need is a blender - small bullet style blenders work best.

2 Pop in the ingredients and blend away till smooth.

3 You may find that after blending the surface of the dressing is quite pale and frothy.

If this is an issue for presentation you can either let it sit a while or cook for 5 minutes or so on the stove until you get a nice red luster.

CREAMY ITALIAN DRESSING

Awesome on pasta or potato salad

INGREDIENTS

2 sundried tomatoes, chopped

3 olives, pitted and chopped

2 tbs tahini

1 tbs lemon juice

¼ cup water

2 tbs almond milk (or plant milk of choice)

2 tsp dried Italian mixed herbs

¼ tsp coarse celtic sea salt, or to taste

Black pepper, to taste

SERVINGS: 1/2 CUP

INSTRUCTIONS

1 Combine all of the ingredients in a bowl or jar with screw top lid and mix together.

CAESAR DRESSING

An Italian favorite you can have everyday

INGREDIENTS

1 cup cashews
1 cup almond milk (or plant milk of choice)
1 tbs lemon juice
1 clove garlic
2 tbs nutritional yeast
½ tsp Dijon mustard
½ tsp coarse celtic sea salt, or to taste
Pepper to taste

SERVINGS: 1 CUP

INSTRUCTIONS

1 Place all ingredients in a blender and blend until creamy.

2 Best served chilled.

CAPER MUSTARD VINAIGRETTE

A green salad's best friend

INGREDIENTS

1 tbs capers, chopped
1 tbs Dijon mustard
1 tbs white vinegar
1 tsp maple syrup
¼ tsp black pepper
2 tbs water
Salt, optional to taste

SERVINGS: 4 - 6

INSTRUCTIONS

1 Combine all of the ingredients in a bowl or jar with screw top lid and mix together.

ORANGE TAHINI DRESSING

Great to dress up a salad or tossed through some noodles!

INGREDIENTS

1 cup orange juice
2 tbs maple syrup
2 tbs tahini
2 tbs tamari (or soy sauce/ Braggs aminos)
1 tsp coarse celtic sea salt
1 tsp sesame oil (optional, leave out for oil free)

SERVINGS: 6

INSTRUCTIONS

1 Combine all of the ingredients in a bowl or jar with screw top lid and mix together.

ASIAN MISO DRESSING

Great over the top of rice, for dipping sushi or spicing up a stir fry.

INGREDIENTS

1 tbs white miso paste
⅓ cup water
2 tsp tamari (or soy sauce/ Braggs aminos)
1 tbs rice wine vinegar
½ tsp coconut sugar
1 nori sheet, crunched up into flakes
Pinch of black pepper
Chili flakes, to taste

SERVINGS: 4 - 6

INSTRUCTIONS

1 Combine all of the ingredients in a bowl or jar with screw top lid and mix together.

CHILI LIME DRESSING

Great with rice, noodles and anything that needs a delicious kick!

INGREDIENTS

2 limes, juiced

1 tsp ginger, grated

1 clove garlic, crushed

½ tsp chili flakes, or to taste

2 tbs tamari (or soy sauce/ Braggs aminos)

2 tsp coconut sugar

½ handful fresh coriander, chopped (or 2 tsp scallions, minced)

½ tsp sesame oil, optional (leave out for oil free)

SERVINGS: 1/3 CUP

INSTRUCTIONS

1 Combine all of the ingredients in a bowl or jar with screw top lid and mix together.

NO "FISH" SAUCE

Ideal for your next Thai curry!

INGREDIENTS

2 tbs coconut aminos (or soy sauce)
½ tsp coconut sugar
1 tbs white miso paste
Pinch of cayenne pepper
1 nori sheet, pulsed up in a coffee grinder
4 tbs water
¼ tsp coarse celtic sea salt, or to taste

SERVINGS: 1/2 CUP

INSTRUCTIONS

1 Combine all of the ingredients in a bowl or jar with screw top lid and mix together.

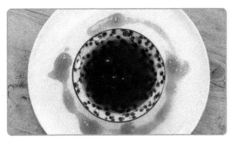

STICKY ORIENTAL REDUCTION

Great as a flavor base in stir-fries or curries.

INGREDIENTS

3 tbs maple syrup

1 tsp tamari (or soy sauce/ Braggs aminos)

3 tbs apricot conserve/ jam/jelly (100% fruit)

SERVINGS: 1/4 CUP

INSTRUCTIONS

1 Place ingredients in a pot or pan and bring to a boil. Reduce heat and simmer until the mixture has thickened.

2 Serve warm or cold.

BALSAMIC GLAZE

Powerful flavor when you need it!

INGREDIENTS

1 cup balsamic vinegar

¼ cup brown sugar (or coconut sugar)

SERVINGS: 1/2 CUP

INSTRUCTIONS

1 Place ingredients in a pot or pan and bring to a boil.

2 Reduce heat and simmer for approximately 20 minutes or until the mixture has reduced by half and coats the back of a spoon.

3 Store at room temperature and use as needed.

PINEAPPLE "HONEY"

Vegan honey... is that even possible? Yes it is!

INGREDIENTS

1 cup pineapple juice
1 cup coconut sugar (or any sugar of your choice)

 RECIPE NOTES

Do not worry if the mixture is a little runny when hot, it does thicken as it cools.

SERVINGS: 0.5 CUPS

INSTRUCTIONS

1. Prepare a pan and stirring spoon. I like to use a non-stick pan so it makes clean up easier.

2. Pour pineapple juice and sugar into pan. Turn heat to medium high and bring mixture to a light boil.

3. Turn down the heat and keep the mixture at a steady simmer. Continue to stir the mixture to keep it smooth and to stop it from burning.

4. After about 15 minutes you will notice that the mixtures become thick and gooey. Once it reaches the consistency you are happy with, remove the pan from the heat and let it sit for a few minutes.

5. Pour into a glass jar... and enjoy!!!

Desserts

Frosted Sweet Potato Cupcakes P137

Chocolate Fudge Cupcake P131

Baked Lemon "Cheesecake" P138

PAPAYA FRUIT SALAD WITH CHIA

This simple papaya fruit salad brings the BEST tastes of Summer to your mouth!

INGREDIENTS

1 large papaya, cut in half lengthways and deseeded

4 chopped dates, or more to taste

1 large banana, sliced

½ cup blueberries (I used frozen, but fresh is best)

1 - 2 tbs chia seeds

SERVINGS: 1 - 2

INSTRUCTIONS

1   Fill your papaya halves with dates, banana and blueberries.

2   Sprinkle chia seeds on top and enjoy!

OVEN ROASTED STONE FRUIT

I am not sure if there is anything better in the world!

INGREDIENTS

1 cinnamon stick
1 tbs lemon juice
¼ cup maple syrup
¼ cup coconut sugar
5 slices of fresh ginger (3mm thick)
1 to 2 vanilla beans, halved (or 2 tsp vanilla extract)
4 nectarines halved and stones remove
2 peaches, halved and stones removed
2 plums, whole
Pinch of salt

SERVINGS: 4

INSTRUCTIONS

1 Place all of the ingredients into an oven proof baking dish.

2 Bake at 175°C/350°F for about 1 hour. Turn every 15 minutes until soft and caramelized.

3 Serve hot with the fruit syrup from the pan (and watch out for the plum stones).

 RECIPE NOTES

Great served with a dollop of coconut cream!

APPLE CRUMBLE

A family classic that tastes just as good vegan style

INGREDIENTS

Main Filling:

6 large apples - peeled, cored and sliced thinly
1 lemon, juiced
1 tbs maple syrup
1 tbs coconut sugar
1 tsp vanilla extract
1 tsp cinnamon
1 cup dried mixed fruit

Crumble Topping:

1 cup whole wheat flour
1 cup oats
½ tsp cinnamon
2 tbs coconut sugar (or sugar of choice)
1 tbs maple syrup
¼ cup apple puree
2 tbs shredded coconut, optional
Pinch of salt

SERVINGS: 4 - 6

INSTRUCTIONS

1 Place all of the main filling ingredients in a pot or pan and cook on a medium high heat until softened.

2 Remove from heat and place mixture into a pie dish (9.5 inch/24cm).

3 Mix the crumble topping ingredients together in a bowl and spread over the top of the fruit mixture. Make sure to cover evenly.

4 Bake in oven at 175°C/350°F for about 20 to 25 minutes or until the top is golden.

5 Serve hot or cold.

RECIPE NOTES

Great served with some coconut cream!

BANANA CREME BRULEE

Indulgent, and utterly delicious!

INGREDIENTS

2 ½ cups almond milk (or plant milk of choice)

3 large ripe bananas

¼ cup chickpea flour (besan flour)

2 tbs cornstarch

¼ tsp coarse celtic sea salt

2 tsp vanilla extract

⅛ tsp turmeric (for color only)

⅓ cup sugar, optional

3 tbs granulated white sugar, for topping/ bruleeing

 RECIPE NOTES

Serve within 10 minutes and do not place back in refrigerator as this will make the topping go soft and runny.

SERVINGS: 6 - 8

INSTRUCTIONS

1 Combine all of the ingredients (except the granulated sugar) in a pot and bring to a simmer over medium to high heat.

2 Continue to stir until the mixture has thickened and feels like a very thick custard.

3 Pour into small cups or ramekins and place in the refrigerator to cool for at least a few hours or until set firm.

4 Spread the sugar over each ramekin in a thin and even layer.

5 If you have a cooking blow torch, use it to carefully melt the sugar and to caramelize it on top.

6 Alternatively, place your ramekins under a broiler/griller and cook until the sugar starts to melt and caramelize on top. Keep a close eye on this so they don't burn.

BANANA CHOC CHIP PAN-CAKE

This stovetop recipe is simple, fast and delicious!

INGREDIENTS

1 cup flour (½ cup whole wheat flour + ½ cup plain)
1 tsp baking powder
1 tsp dry instant yeast
1 tsp coarse celtic sea salt
1 tsp maple syrup
1 cup water

Topping Suggestions:
Peanut butter, maple syrup, chocolate chips, banana, apple puree, dried fruit (soaked), vanilla extract, cinnamon, fruit, pears, vegan marshmallows, coconut sugar, dollops of coconut cream etc.

 RECIPE NOTES

I like to use banana, chocolate chips, coconut sugar, maple syrup and dollops of coconut cream when cooking. Once done, top with extra coconut sugar, maple syrup and chocolate chips. This is a very decadent and only a once in a while treat.

SERVINGS: 4

INSTRUCTIONS

1 Place all of the ingredients in a non-stick frying pan (do not put on stove top yet). Stir gently with a rubber spatula or back of a wooden spoon. Flatten mixture out evenly in the pan to form your pan-cake.

2 Add toppings.

3 Cover the pan with a lid making sure that it is tightly closed for 5 minutes . Place on medium to high heat.

4 Open vents or tilt lid slightly so a little bit of air and moisture can escape. Lower heat to medium and continue to cook for another 15 minutes or until cooked through.

5 Take off heat. Remove lid. Gently remove pan-cake and serve hot. I like to serve on a wooden board as it helps keep the base nice and firm.

CHOCOLATE FUDGE CUP CAKE

A quick chocolate cake fix whenever you need it.

INGREDIENTS

3 tbs almond milk (or plant milk of choice)
1 tbs maple syrup (or 3 pitted dates)
½ tsp vanilla extract
2 tbs whole wheat flour
¼ tsp baking powder
1 tbs cocoa powder
Pinch of salt
Vegan choc chips for on top once cooked (optional)

RECIPE NOTES

If you prefer not to use a microwave, you can bake in oven until the top is firm and cooked through. Be sure to use a ramekin or oven proof mug.

SERVINGS: 1

INSTRUCTIONS

1 If using dates, blend first with the liquid ingredients. Otherwise, mix all ingredients in a large mug until a batter forms.

2 Microwave for 1 minute. If too soft, microwave for another 10 seconds at a time until done. The top should bounce back when you touch it.

3 Top with chocolate chips if wanted. Enjoy!

CHOCOLATE FUDGE BROWNIES

These are even better the day after they are made - if they last that long!

INGREDIENTS

Fudge:

20 dates (soaked in juice of 1 lemon + enough water to cover, soak at least 1 hour and drain, reserve liquid)*

½ cup of the date soaking liquid

* keep remaining liquid for smoothies etc

2 tsp vanilla extract

1¼ tsp coarse celtic sea salt

½ cup maple syrup

Chocolate Mix:

1 ½ cups whole wheat flour

½ cup cocoa powder

1 tsp baking soda

½ cup plant milk (almond/soy/oat/rice/coconut)

Optional Extras:

¼ cup vegan chocolate chips

¼ cup chopped walnuts

SERVINGS: 8 - 12

INSTRUCTIONS

1 Blend the fudge ingredients in a blender until smooth. Reserve ½ cup of the mixture and add the rest to a mixing bowl.

2 Add in the chocolate mix ingredients and mix until well combined.

3 Pour into 20cm/8 inch square cake pan lined with non-stick parchment paper.

4 Top with the reserved fudge mixture and swirl through with a skewer or a fork to lightly combine and add a pattern on top.

5 Bake at 175°C/350°F for 45 minutes or until a skewer comes out clean. Let cool for several hours or overnight in the refrigerator.

 RECIPE NOTES

Serve with a dollop of coconut cream or vegan ice cream.

CHOC CHIP COOKIES
You will have to fight the kids for these!

INGREDIENTS

1 cup wholemeal flour or your flour of choice
1 tsp baking powder
1 tsp baking soda
½ tsp coarse celtic sea salt
¼ cup coconut sugar or your favorite sweetener
100 ml/3.38 fl oz rice milk (or plant milk of choice)
5 whole medjool dates
2 tsp vanilla extract
½ cup vegan chocolate broken up into chips

SERVINGS: 12 - 16 COOKIES

INSTRUCTIONS

1 For this recipe you will need a large mixing bowl and spoon, a baking tray lined with non-stick parchment paper and a small blender.

2 First of all add your dry ingredients excluding salt & chocolate to your mixing bowl, then mix together. Now is a good time to get your oven on and set to 175°C/350°F.

3 For the next stage add your dates, vanilla extract, celtic sea salt and rice milk to a blender and blend till smooth.

4 Now add the blended mixture and chocolate to the dry ingredients and mix thoroughly.

5 Use an ice-cream scoop or suitable spoon to evenly place dollops of cookie dough on your lined baking tray.

6 Pop your cookies in the oven for approximately 12 minutes or until golden brown.

7 Leave the cookies to cool for 5-10 minutes before serving to the hungry hordes!

GLUTEN FREE BANANA BREAD

Gluten Free, delicious and easy to make!

INGREDIENTS

Dry Ingredients

1 ¾ cups brown rice flour
¼ cup potato flour
¼ cup coconut sugar
2 tsp baking soda
1 tsp cinnamon

Wet Ingredients

3 small bananas mashed
½ cup apple puree
3 tbs maple syrup
1 tsp vanilla extract

 RECIPE NOTES

This makes one banana loaf and can be kept at room temperature or in refrigerator in an air tight container for about a week.

INSTRUCTIONS

1 Preheat oven to 175°C/350°F.

2 Line a 9 × 5 inch bread loaf pan with non-stick parchment paper.

3 Place all the dry ingredients in a mixing bowl and stir until well combined.

4 Pour all wet ingredients on top of the dry and gently mix through until just combined. Don't over mix.

5 Pour batter into the loaf pan and bake in middle of oven for approximately 45 minutes. Check that the center is cooked by using a skewer or chop stick, making sure that it comes out clean. If not, bake for 5 or 10 minutes longer.

6 Gently remove from loaf pan and turn onto a wire cooling rack. Leave for about an hour until it has completely cooled. This will make it easy to cut so the loaf does not fall apart.

STICKY DATE MUFFINS

Tastes just like sticky date pudding, but without the eggs, dairy and fat!

INGREDIENTS

Dry Ingredients
½ cup oats (I used quick oats)
¼ cup whole wheat flour
2 tsp baking powder
¼ cup coconut sugar

Wet Ingredients
1 cup water
1 tsp vanilla extract
15 whole medjool dates pitted
2 whole bananas

SERVINGS: 12 MUFFINS

INSTRUCTIONS

1 Preheat oven to 175°C/350°F.

2 Before you begin you will need a blender/ food processor for the wet ingredients, a mixing bowl and spatula/ mixing spoon, a muffin baking tray lined with non-stick parchment paper or silicone muffin cups.

3 Next, get all the dry ingredients together in a mixing bowl and mix thoroughly.

4 Blend all the wet ingredients together in your blender/food processor. It is fine to leave some date texture in the mixture as those bite size pieces taste great in the finished muffin!

5 Pour the wet ingredient mix into the dry ingredient mixing bowl and fold the mixture together. Keep folding gently using your spatula to scrape any dry bits stuck to the side of the bowl.

6 Once the mixture is nicely mixed it's time to fill up the muffin cups. I used an ice cream scoop as it made it easy to use a consistent amount of mixture. These muffins do not rise much so you can fill the cups almost to the top.

7 Place the muffin tray in the oven for 25 minutes or until cooked through. Once cooked, let cool for 20 minutes before eating. Bon Appetit!

NO BAKE CARROT CAKE MUFFINS

Moist, sweet and filling!

SERVINGS: 10 MUFFINS

INGREDIENTS

1 ¼ cups nuts (eg. walnuts, pecans, brazil nuts etc)
1 cup desiccated coconut
2 medium carrots, peeled
4 large dates, pitted
¼ cup raisins (or other dried fruit)
1 tbs oats
⅛ tsp ground nutmeg
¼ tsp ground ginger
¼ tsp ground cinnamon
1 piece orange rind, optional

Icing:
½ cup cashews
½ tbs maple syrup
2 tsp lemon juice
¼ tsp vanilla extract

Optional toppings:
Walnuts, shredded coconut

INSTRUCTIONS

1 Place all of the main ingredients in a food processor and process until well combined.

2 Using a silicone muffin cup, shape the mixture into muffins. Or shape by hand into any shape you like.

3 Next, add the icing ingredients into a small blender and blend until smooth and creamy.

4 Add icing evenly to the tops of the carrot cake muffins.

5 Sprinkle with walnuts and shredded coconut if you like.

FROSTED SWEET POTATO CUPCAKES

The peanut butter frosting just lifts these delicious cupcakes to another level!

INGREDIENTS

Cupcakes:

1 cup plant milk (almond/soy/rice/coconut)
10 dates or ½ cup coconut sugar
1 tsp white vinegar
1¼ cups flour (spelt/all purpose/plain)
1 tbs cornstarch
1 tsp baking powder
½ tsp coarse celtic sea salt
1 cup cooked and mashed sweet potatoes
2 tsp vanilla extract

Peanut Butter Frosting:

3 tbs peanut butter
100g cooked sweet potato
½ tbs lemon juice
1 tbs maple syrup
Pinch of salt

Optional Extra:

Drizzle maple syrup over the top when serving

RECIPE NOTES

Add 1 to 2 tbs cocoa powder for chocolate cupcakes.

SERVINGS: 12 CUPCAKES

INSTRUCTIONS

1 If using dates, blend the dates and the plant milk together in a blender until smooth. Combine all cupcake ingredients together in a mixing bowl until well combined.

2 Pour into lined cupcake tins or cups and fill each cup about three quarters of the way.

3 Bake at 175°C/350°F for 20 to 25 minutes until done. Remove from oven and let them totally cool down before frosting them.

4 For the frosting, combine all of the frosting ingredients in a small mixing bowl and use a fork or whisk to combine well. Keep mixing until it has a nice frosting consistency.

5 Evenly spread the frosting over each muffin using a spatula or spoon.

6 Serve immediately or keep them in the refrigerator in a covered container until ready to serve.

BAKED LEMON "CHEESECAKE"

Harking back to my German heritage!

INGREDIENTS

Base:
5 dates, pitted
½ cup almond meal (not flour)
½ cup oats

Filling:
1 tbs white miso paste
⅓ cup chickpea flour
½ cup cashews
½ cup oats
1 cup plant milk (soy/almond/rice/coconut)
¼ cup lemon juice
1 tsp vanilla extract
½ tsp coarse celtic sea salt
¼ cup white sugar
3 tbs vegan custard powder (or cornstarch)
250g/8.75oz firm silken tofu, rinsed and drained

SERVINGS: 8

INSTRUCTIONS

1 Place base ingredients in a food processor and blend until the mixture sticks together. Put into the base of a 20cm spring form cake tin that has been lined with nonstick parchment paper. Press down so it forms an even base for the cake.

2 Next, prepare the filling by placing all of the filling ingredients in a food processor. Process until well combined and smooth.

3 Pour mixture over the base.

4 Bake at 200°C/400°F for 30 minutes, then 180°C/360°F for 20 minutes.

5 Let cool completely overnight to allow it to set firm.

6 Serve chilled.

MANGO "CHEESECA[

Smooth and light - very easy to say yes to a second piece!

INGREDIENTS

Base:
1 cup oats
8 dates, pitted
1 tsp vanilla extract

Filling:
3 cups plant milk
(almond/soy/rice/
coconut)
1 cup almonds, blanched
2 tbs lemon juice
1 tsp coarse celtic sea salt
2 tbs coconut sugar
1 cup mango flesh
(200g/7oz)
1 tbs agar agar powder
2 tsp tapioca starch
1 cup hot boiled water
2 tsp vanilla extract
½ tsp white miso paste,
optional

Optional toppings:
Sliced mango and
passionfruit

RECIPE NOTES

Great served with a dollop of
coconut cream!

SERVINGS: 8

INSTRUCTIONS

1 Place base ingredients in a food processor and blend until the mixture sticks together. Put into the base of a 20cm/9" spring form cake tin that has been lined with nonstick parchment paper. Press down so it forms an even base for the cake. Wet your hands a little bit if the mixture sticks to you.

2 Next, prepare the mango filling by placing all of the filling ingredients in a food processor. Again, process until well combined and smooth.

3 Place the filling mixture in a pot and cook for 10 minutes over medium high heat to activate the agar.

4 Pour the mixture over the base and let it set in the refrigerator overnight. It must be completely cooled down so it sets firm.

5 Decorate with mango and passionfruit if you wish.

6 Carefully remove from the cake tin and serve.

CARAMELIZED PEAR CAKE

Another European classic. Perfect with tea or coffee.

INGREDIENTS

Base Wet:
220g/8oz apple puree
2 tsp vanilla essence
⅔ cup plant milk (almond/coconut)
10 dates, pitted
¼ cup maple syrup

Base Dry:
3 tbs chickpea flour (besan flour)
2 ½ cups flour (I used white spelt)
2 tsp baking powder
1 tsp coarse celtic sea salt
½ cup desiccated coconut
⅓ cup coconut sugar

Filling:
200g/7oz sliced pears (tinned is fine)
1 tsp cinnamon
¼ cup coconut sugar

Topping:
1 cup cashews
1 tbs pinenuts
2 tsp white vinegar (or lemon juice)
½ cup water (or pear juice)

SERVINGS: 6 - 8

INSTRUCTIONS

1 Blend or process the base wet ingredients together till smooth.

2 Pour mixture into a bowl and mix in the base dry ingredients. Mix together until well combined.

3 Lightly press into a 23cm/9" square cake tin that has been lined with non-stick parchment paper. Bake at 180°C/360°F for 15 minutes.

4 Place the pears evenly over the base. Mix the cinnamon and sugar and keep 2 tbs worth of the mixture aside. Sprinkle the cinnamon and sugar mix over the top of the pears.

5 Blend the topping ingredients until smooth and pour over the top of the pears. Sprinkle with reserved cinnamon and sugar mix.

6 Return to the oven and bake for another 25 to 30 minutes until set and cooked through. Check with a skewer or toothpick and make sure it comes out clean.

7 Let cool for at least one hour before serving. Or serve chilled.

RECIPE NOTES

Great served with some coconut cream!

140

NO BAKE STRAWBERRY CAKE

A great summer afternoon cake. Kids love it too!

INGREDIENTS

Base:
- 1 cup oats
- 8 large dates, pitted
- 1 tsp vanilla extract

Strawberry Filling:
- 3 cups oats
- 1 cup plant milk (almond/soy/rice/coconut)
- 50ml lemon juice
- ¼ cup maple syrup
- 1 tsp vanilla extract
- 1kg/2.2pounds strawberries (reserve some for decorating)
- ½ cup water
- 1 tbs agar agar powder
- ¼ cup sugar, optional

Topping:
Passionfruit + Strawberries

RECIPE NOTES

Great served with some coconut cream!

SERVINGS: 8

INSTRUCTIONS

1 Place base ingredients in a food processor and blend until the mixture sticks together.

2 Put into the base of a 20cm spring form cake tin that has been lined with nonstick parchment paper. Press down so it forms an even base for the cake. Wet your hands a little bit if the mixture sticks to you.

3 Next, prepare the strawberry filling by placing all of the filling ingredients in a food processor. Again, process until well combined and smooth.

4 Put the filling mixture in a large pot and cook on medium heat for 10 minutes until the mixture is really thick. It will resemble very thick porridge.

5 Pour the filling over the base and smooth out so the top is flat.

6 Set in refrigerator to cool for several hours or overnight so it sets.

7 Decorate with passionfruit and strawberries.

8 Remove from cake tin and serve.

APPLE STRUDEL RICE PAPER ROLLS

These delicious apple strudel rice paper rolls take a sweet twist to create a special dessert!

INGREDIENTS

Apple Strudel Ingredients:

3 small apples peeled, cored ad thinly sliced (approximately 500g/15oz)

1½ tbs lemon juice (juice of 1 small lemon)

¼ cup mixed dried fruit you can use any you like

2-3 tbs coconut sugar

1 tsp cinnamon

¼ cup almond meal or instant rolled oats

1 packet rice paper sheets

Vanilla Sauce Ingredients:

3 cups plant milk (eg almond, soy, rice, oat)

1 tbs vanilla extract

3 tbs cornstarch or arrowroot (use more cornstarch if you want the sauce thicker)

⅛ tsp turmeric (to make the sauce more yellow)

1 tbs white sugar, optional or to taste

 RECIPE NOTES

Sprinkle with cinnamon, dried fruit or some maple syrup for some extra zip!!!

SERVINGS: 8 ROLLS

INSTRUCTIONS

1 Mix all of the ingredients for the strudel mixture (except the rice paper) and put in a pot or pan. Cook over medium heat for about 5 minutes until slightly softened and caramelized. Remove from heat and set aside to cool in the refrigerator.

2 Place all of the vanilla sauce ingredients in a pot and heat over medium for about 5 to 10 minutes, stirring constantly until slightly thickened.

Note: If you want a thicker custard like consistency, just add more cornstarch during the cooking process.

3 Remove from heat and serve hot or let cool.

4 Soak rice paper sheet in water for about 30 seconds until soft and pliable. Place on a damp tea towel to make it easier to work with. Spoon a tablespoon full of mixture onto the bottom third of the rice paper. Fold the sides in slightly, then roll up from the bottom like a spring roll.

5 Place all completed rolls onto some parchment paper to avoid them sticking together.

6 Serve the apple strudel rolls in a bowl full of vanilla sauce or top with vanilla sauce. YUM!

CHOCOLATE CARAMEL DIPPING SAUCE

Delicious, indulgent and tasty without fat or oil!

INGREDIENTS

1 cup sweet potato (kumara) cubed and boiled or steamed

3 whole medjool dates pitted and soaked in 3tbs hot water

1 tsp coarse celtic sea salt

1 tsp vanilla extract

3 tsp cocoa powder unsweetened

¼ cup maple syrup

SERVINGS: 1 - 1.5 CUPS

INSTRUCTIONS

1 All you need for this recipe is a blender. I used a small bullet style blender.

2 Add the sweet potato first, then the rest of the ingredients and blend for approximately 1 minute.

2 MINUTE CHOC ORANGE MOUSSE

Mmmmm Chocolate and Orange... what a winning combination!

INGREDIENTS

1 avocado
1 tsp vanilla extract
1-2 tbs maple syrup
1 tbs cocoa powder
(I used raw organic)
¼ - ½ cup orange juice

SERVINGS: 1 - 2

INSTRUCTIONS

1 All you need for this recipe is a blender.

2 Put all the ingredients in and blend until smooth.

Note: These ingredients are a guide only. You can change the texture and flavors to suit your own tastes.

FESTIVE ICE CREAM LOG

*Perfect on a hot summer's afternoon
splashed with maple syrup*

INGREDIENTS

735g/26oz frozen bananas
2 tsp vanilla extract
1 cup almond milk or
coconut milk

Add Ins:
1 cup mixed dried fruit

RECIPE NOTES

Great with cherries mixed through. I use a "cooking" shower cap to stretch over the top because it is easy to work with and nice and thick - better than cling film because it doesn't stick or break.

SERVINGS: 6 - 8

INSTRUCTIONS

1 Line an 8.5 × 4.5 × 2.5 inch bread loaf tin with non-stick parchment paper. You can also use a silicon bread pan.

2 Place all of the ingredients (except the add ins) into a food processor for approximately 20 to 30 seconds until smooth and well combined.

3 Pour this mixture into a bowl and stir through the dried fruit until well mixed.

4 Pour into lined loaf tin and push down and spread evenly on top till smooth and as flat as possible.

5 Cover with some more non-stick parchment paper or very thick plastic and place it on top.

   Push down so the plastic touches the ice cream and stops air from getting in.

   Put a rubber band around the edge to seal on.

6 Place in freezer until firm and ready to serve. Can be made days or weeks ahead.

7 Let thaw for about 20 minutes prior to serving to make cutting easier.

8 Remove and cut to serve.

INDEX

2 Ingredient Pancakes   19
2 Ingredients Waffles   18
2 Minute Choc Orange Mousse   144
5 Minute Curry Sauce   108

A
Almond "Cheese"   73
Almond Chai Latte   27
Almond Parmesan "Cheese"   95
Apple Crumble   128
Apple Strudel Rice Paper Rolls   142
Asian Miso Dressing   118
Asian Water chestnut Noodle Stir Fry   64
Asparagus Puffs   86

B
Baked Lemon "Cheesecake"   138
Baked Rice Paper Pockets   65
Baklava Quinoa Porridge   12
Balsamic Glaze   122
Banana Choc Chip Pan-Cake   130
Banana Creme Brulee   129
Blend, Heat and Eat Tomato Soup   43
Breakfast Couscous Bites   17

C
Cabbage Terrine   41
Caesar Dressing   115
Caper Mustard Vinaigrette   116
Caramelized Pear Cake   140
Cashew "Cheese"   72
Cashew Sour Cream   101
Char grilled Red Pepper Pesto   96
Chickpea Omelette   23
Chili Lime Dressing   119
Chili Tofu Lettuce Cups   87
Choc Chip Cookies   133
Chocolate Caramel Dipping Sauce   143
Chocolate Fudge Brownies   132
Chocolate Fudge Cup Cake   131
Coconut Chia Fruit Bowl   20
Creamed Vanilla Rice Pudding   10
Creamy Cauliflower   82

Creamy Garlic Sauce   107
Creamy Italian Dressing   114
Creamy Lemon Dijon Potato Salad   81
Creamy Potato Broccoli Bake   36
Creamy Pumpkin Mint Pea Risotto   45
Crumbed "No Fish" Fillets   55
Curried Singapore Noodles   61
Curry Fried Rice   62

D
Dumplings in Hearty Asian Broth   66

E
Eggplant Bolognese   51
"Eggy" Breakfast Muffins   21

F
Festive Ice Cream Log   145
Frosted Sweet Potato Cupcakes   137

G
Gluten Free Banana Bread   134
Gluten Free Quinoa Crusted Pizza   32
Greek Spiced Eggplant Hummus   89
Greek Style Herbed Koftas   56
Guacamole   99

H
Halloumi "Cheese"   75
Hearty Mushroom Lentil Burgers   39
Herbed Mashed Potatoes   78
Hoisin Sauce   111
Homemade Baked Beans   24
Homemade Gnocchi   37
Homemade Marinara Sauce   50

I
Instant Cheesy Herb & Garlic Sauce   106

J
Jackfruit Peri Peri Skewers + Salsa   59

L

Lasagne Roll Up Bake   40
Lasagne Style Potato Bake   46
Lemon and Blueberry Muffins   26
Lemon Potatoes   80

M

Mac and "Cheese"   33
Mango "Cheesecake"   139
Maple Spiced Oven Roasted Nuts   91
Mediterranean Polenta Stacks   35
Middle Eastern Cauliflower   83
Mini Quiches   85
Mushroom Gravy   105

N

No "Fish" Sauce   120
No Bake Carrot Cake Muffins   136
No Bake Strawberry Cake   141
No Cook Asian Stir Fry   63
No Cook Buckwheat Porridge   13
No Knead Pizza   31
No Oil Hummus   88
No Oil Seasoned Fries   77
Nut Free "Cheese" Sauce   76
Nut Free Smoked Paprika "Cheese"   74

O

Oil Free Vegan Mayonnaise   100
One Pot Mexican Rice   58
Onion Gravy   104
Orange Tahini Dressing   117
Oven Roasted Baked Potatoes   79
Oven Roasted Stone Fruit   127

P

Papaya Fruit Salad with Chia   126
Peanut Dipping Sauce   110
Pineapple "Honey"   123
Pizza in a Pan   30
Polenta Porridge with Apricot Drizzle   11
Potato and Lentil Dahl   60
Potato and Vegetable Polenta Slice   53
Potato Crusted Quiche   34
Potato Hash Browns   22

Q

Quick Start Smoothies   8

R

Rich Brown Gravy   103
Rustic Bread Sticks   90

S

Salt Free Garlic & Herb Seasoning   94
Satay Noodles   69
Savory French Toast   15
Shepherd's Pie   48
Smokey Leek and Potato Soup   44
Smoky Red Bell Pepper Dip   98
Soy Yogurt   9
Spiced Pumpkin Soup + Cashew   42
Spicy Tomato Ketchup   109
Sticky Date Muffins   135
Sticky Oriental Reduction   121
Stuffed Mushrooms   49
Stuffed Red Peppers   54
Sunflower Seed Falafels   57
Sweet Chili Chutney   112
Sweet Chili Dressing   113
Sweet French Toast   14
Sweet Potato Falafel Burgers   38

T

Thai Red Curry   67
Tofu Scramble   16
Tofu Scramble Fried Rice   68
Tzatziki   97

V

Vegan Ground "Beef"   47
Vegetable Black Bean Loaf   52
Vegetable Parcels   84

W

White Sauce   102

Z

Zucchini and Corn Fritters   25

7 DAILY MEAL PLANS

DAY 1: HEALTHY DAY MEAL PLAN

Breakfast: High Energy Breakfast Smoothie *8*
Lunch: Chili Tofu Lettuce Cups *87*
Dinner: Potato and Lentil Dahl with Rice *60*
Dessert: Almond Chai Latte *27*

DAY 2: WEIGHT LOSS DAY MEAL PLAN

Breakfast: Tofu Scramble *16*
Lunch: Blend, Heat and Eat Tomato Soup *43*
Dinner: Vegetable Parcels *84*
Dessert: Papaya Fruit Salad with Chia *126*

DAY 3: ITALIAN LOVERS MEAL PLAN

Breakfast: Zucchini Corn Fritters *25*
Lunch: Mac & Cheese *33*
Dinner: Pizza in a Pan *30*
Dessert: 2 Minute Choc Orange Mousse *144*

DAY 4: JAPANESE DAY MEAL PLAN

Breakfast: No-Cook Buckwheat Porridge *13*
Lunch: No Cook Asian Stir-fry *63*
Dinner: Dumplings in Hearty Asian Broth *66*
Dessert: Oven Roasted Stone Fruit *127*

DAY 5: INDULGENT DAY MEAL PLAN

Breakfast: Sweet or Savory French Toast *15*
Lunch: Hearty Mushroom Lentil Burgers *39*
Dinner: Potato Crusted Quiche *34*
Dessert: Chocolate Fudge Cup Cake *131*

DAY 6: COMFORT FOOD DAY MEAL PLAN

Breakfast: Creamed Vanilla Rice Pudding *10*
Lunch: Smoky Leek and Potato Soup *44*
Dinner: Quiche *85*
Dessert: Apple Crumble *128*

DAY 7: LAZY DAY MEAL PLAN - 8 INGREDIENTS OR LESS

Breakfast: Date Banana Porridge Smoothie *8*
Lunch: Satay Noodles *69*
Dinner: Homemade Marinara Sauce with Pasta *50*
Dessert: Chocolate Caramel Dipping Sauce with Strawberries *143*